# 100 GREATS

# SUSSEX
## COUNTY CRICKET CLUB

*June 2001: Murray Goodwin (201\*) and Richard Montgomerie (160\*) add 372 for 0 wickets against Nottinghamshire at Trent Bridge. This is the second highest opening partnership for Sussex and the third highest for any wicket in the County's history.*

# 100 GREATS

# SUSSEX
## COUNTY CRICKET CLUB

WRITTEN BY
JOHN WALLACE

TEMPUS

First published 2002
Copyright © John Wallace, 2002

Tempus Publishing Limited
The Mill, Brimscombe Port,
Stroud, Gloucestershire, GL5 2QG

ISBN 0 7524 2421 1

Typesetting and origination by
Tempus Publishing Limited
Printed in Great Britain by
Midway Colour Print, Wiltshire

**Statistical Note:**

All career statistics, based substantially on the information from the Association of Cricket Statisticians booklet, are correct to April 2002 and refer to performances for Sussex CCC since 1815 in first-class cricket, including County Championship matches, 'friendlies' between the wars, matches against touring sides, together with limited-overs matches in Gillette (GC), NatWest (NWT), Benson and Hedges (B&H) and Cheltenham and Gloucester (C&G) cup ties. I have not sought to distinguish between the various sponsors for the Sunday League and use the abbreviation (SL), although I am aware that nowadays some matches are not played on Sundays. Statistics shown in italics refer to limited-overs matches. To accommodate the problems of 4, 5, 6 and 8 ball overs in first-class cricket I have rounded up or down the number of overs bowled as I dislike the idea of showing only the number of balls bowled. Career best performances refer to those for Sussex; some players, of course, have produced better figures when not playing for the County!

**Key:**
RHB – right-handed batsman
LHB – left-handed batsman
RF/LF – right/left-arm fast
RFM/LFM – right/left-arm fast medium
RMF/LMF – right/left-arm medium fast
RM/LM – right/left-arm medium pace
RSM – right slow-medium
SRA – slow round arm
OB – off-spinner
SLA – slow left-arm spinner
SMLA – slow-medium left-arm
LB(G) – leg-break (and googly) bowler
WK – wicketkeeper

# PREFACE

When I was about to write this book I mentioned it to a Yorkshire friend who replied with a certain irony common to people from that region that there had never been 100 great Sussex cricketers. 'Nor Yorkshire ones either,' I retorted somewhat curtly. The word 'great' in the sporting context is certainly grossly overused and I doubt whether my friend could find half that number in his county. However, I take pleasure in the fact that Sussex has surely produced some very great players – from C.B. Fry and Ranji in the early days through Maurice Tate, Arthur Gilligan and the Langridge and Parks families to Ted Dexter, and perhaps Tony Greig in later years. I have interpreted my task as producing some short biographies not only of great players, but also of those who have been great servants of Sussex County Cricket Club. These range from men like Albert Relf, Joe Vine, George Cox father and son, Robin Marlar and Ian Thomson, who did not receive their due in Test match terms, to some much less well-known and to others, such as Billy Griffith, who were Sussex men and made a great contribution to the game as a whole.

Any compilation of this sort is, of course, bound to arouse some controversy when it comes to selection. I have cheated a little by including the two Hide brothers on one page, but I have listened to many friends and lovers of Sussex cricket and made some adjustments according to some of their suggestions. The final choice, however, was mine and remains my own responsibility.

# ACKNOWLEDGEMENTS

I am most grateful to Ted Dexter, former Sussex and England captain and currently president of MCC, for writing the foreword and to James Howarth, Kate Wiseman and Rosie Knowles of Tempus Publishing for their ready help and guidance. I am deeply indebted to Rob Boddie, honorary librarian at Sussex County Cricket Club, for the loan of all sorts of material and for his constant interest and encouragement, and to Roger Packham for reading the text and making a host of valuable suggestions. My thanks go also to Neil Beck for his help with limited-overs statistics and to Gordon Potter for comments on players of the 1950s. For the loan of photographs I am indebted to Nicholas Sharp, John Fowling, Francesca Watson, and *The Cricketer* magazine. For the use of photographs I acknowledge 'Allsport' (particularly for those of Chris Adams), Bill Smith, and George Herringshaw (*www.sporting-heroes.net*) and to others whose photographs may have been used inadvertently without acknowledgement.

John Wallace
Langton Green
April 2002

# BIBLIOGRAPHY

*Wisden Cricketers' Almanack* (relevant editions)
*Sussex County Cricket Handbook* (relevant editions)
*The Playfair Cricket Annual* (relevant editions)
*The Cricketer* (relevant editions)
Sussex County Cricket Club: *Hove and Away* magazines
Benny Green: *The Wisden Book of Cricketers' Lives* (Macdonald Queen Anne Press, 1986)
Christopher Martin-Jenkins: *World Cricketers* (Oxford University Press, 1996)
Alan Hill: *The Family Fortune* (Scan Books, 1978)
W.H. Frindall: *The Wisden Book of Test Cricket* (Macdonald and Jane's, 1979)
Christopher Lee: *From the Sea End* (Partridge Press, 1989)
John Marshall: *Sussex Cricket* (Heinemann, 1959)
E.W. Swanton: *Cricketers of my Time* (André Deutsch, 1999)
David Frith: *Silence of the Heart* (Mainstream Publishing, 2001)
George Washer: *A Complete Record of Sussex County Cricket 1728-1957*

# SUSSEX'S GREATEST PLAYERS?

A recent poll of twelve former Sussex players produced the following team:

1. D.S. Sheppard*
2. John Langridge
3. K.S. Ranjitsinhji
4. E.R. Dexter
5. C.B. Fry
6. J.M. Parks**
7. James Langridge
8. Imran Khan
9. M.W. Tate
10. J.A. Snow
11. N.I. Thomson

Twelfth man: R.G. Marlar

*captain
** wicketkeeper

Some Sussex members have commented that K.S. Duleepsinhji, Albert Relf, Arthur Gilligan (a captain of great ability) and Tony Greig might well have been included in the team, but there is, sadly, only room for eleven men!

# FOREWORD

## BY TED DEXTER

Just to read the list of cricketers' names is enough to set the pulse racing of anyone who has been close to Sussex cricket for whatever reason.

John Wallace is a writer who is skilled in maintaining structure and balance when there is so much material available about this galaxy of talent. And it is not just the greats like Tate, the two 'Sinhjis', Imran Khan, John Snow, Pataudi, Fry and many others who catch the attention. There are the real bedrock names of Langridge, Parks, Cornford, Cox and Gilligan that bring the warmest emotions to the surface.

Of course, on a personal note, I have been interested to see what this historian has had to say about my immediate contemporaries and others I have got to know in later years like Sheppard, Doggart, the Buss brothers and that mainstay of the team that I had the privilege to captain in the sixties, Ian Thomson.

I was at the County Ground again the other day and the conversation got round to the vagaries of the pitch as affected by sea frets or tidal conditions. It reminded me of what a lucky chance it was for me to play at Hove where, depending on the day and even on the time of day, the pitch could favour either the bat or the ball quite markedly.

There have been many theories about why the ball should move about so erratically, but Ian Thomson knew instinctively when was the time to bowl and when not. Even on the brightest morning, as late as the 11.30 a.m. start of those days, with the slightest sea breeze over his left shoulder, running up the hill, there could be juicy pitch marks for well over the hour – only to finish as abruptly as they appeared. Then all was benign. Until, that is, the eagle-eyed Thomson would sense a change around five o'clock in the evening, often coinciding with the new ball in those days when overs were bowled so much more quickly. As the best bowler in the side, he was entitled to bowl whenever it suited him and no captain would begrudge him a quiet time in the outfield in-between.

I could reminisce in this fashion about all those people I was lucky enough to share the field with. Better for an expert to put us all into context so that we can enjoy the whole.

# 100 SUSSEX GREATS

Chris Adams
Bill Athey
John Barclay
Hugh Bartlett
Don Bates
George Bean
Michael Bevan
Cyril Bland
Ted Bowley
Tom Box
George Brann
Tony Buss
Mike Buss
Harry Butt
Herbert Chaplin
Tommy Cook
Jim Cornford
'Tich' Cornford
George Cox senior
George Cox junior
Ted Dexter
Michael Di Venuto
Hubert Doggart
K.S. Duleepsinhji
Charles Fry
Arthur Gilligan
Harold Gilligan
Murray Goodwin
Ian Gould
Peter Graves
Tony Greig
Ian Greig
'Billy' Griffith
Mike Griffith

'Jim' Hammond
Arthur & Jesse Hide
'Jack' Holmes
Walter Humphreys
Imran Khan
Ted James
Javed Miandad
Vallance Jupp
Ernest Killick
James Kirtley
James Langridge
John Langridge
Richard Langridge
George Leach
Les Lenham
Neil Lenham
Garth le Roux
Jason Lewry
William Lillywhite
James Lillywhite junior
Arnold Long
Robin Marlar
Alan Melville
Gehan Mendis
Richard Montgomerie
Peter Moores
William Murdoch
William Newham
Charlie Oakes
Alan Oakman
Paul Parker
Harry Parks
James Horace Parks
James Michael Parks

Nawab of Pataudi
Harry Phillips
Tony Pigott
K.S. Ranjitsinhji
Dermot Reeve
Albert Relf
Robert Relf
Ian Salisbury
Lord David Sheppard
Sir C. Aubrey Smith
Charles Smith
David Smith
Donald Smith
John Snow
James Southerton
John Spencer
George Street
Ken Suttle
Fred Tate
Maurice Tate
Ian Thomson
Joe Vine
Chris Waller
Rupert Webb
Alan Wells
Colin Wells
Bert Wensley
Kepler Wessels
Herbert Wilson
John Wisden
Jim Wood
Richard Young

The top twenty, who appear here in italics, occupy two pages instead of the usual one.

# Christopher J. Adams

*RHB & RM/OB, 1998-*

**Born:** Whitwell, Derbyshire, 6 May 1970

**County Cap:** 1998
**County Captain:** 1998-

**Batting Record:**

| M | I | NO | Runs | Avge |
|---|---|----|------|------|
| 66 | 109 | 9 | 4,129 | 41.29 |
| *72* | *71* | *10* | *2,747* | *45.03* |

| 100 | 50 | | CT/St |
|-----|----|--|-------|
| 9 | 23 | | 94 |
| *6* | *20* | | *37* |

**Bowling Record:**

| O | M | Runs | W | Avge |
|---|---|------|---|------|
| 218 | 42 | 663 | 22 | 30.13 |
| *148.4* | *3* | *735* | *26* | *28.27* |

| 5wI | 10wM |
|-----|------|
| - | - |
| *1* | *-* |

**Career Best Performances:**
192 v. Derbyshire, Arundel, 2001
11.2-2-28-4 v. Durham, Chester-le-Street, 2001
*163 v. Middlesex, Arundel, 1999 (SL)*
*5.2-0-16-5 v. Middlesex, Hove, 1998 (SL)*

Chris Adams represented English and MCC Schools as a boy and England Young Cricketers in 1989, a year after he made his first-class debut for Derbyshire. Educated at Chesterfield Boys' Grammar School and Repton School, he was an outstanding schoolboy cricketer and very proud to have beaten Richard Hutton's twenty-five-year-old record in a Repton season – 1,242 runs at an average of 73 in 1987. He made his Championship debut against Surrey in 1988 and started to make his mark two seasons later. He began the season with 111 not out against Cambridge University and went on to score 800 Championship runs, including 101 against Yorkshire at Scarborough. By 1992 he was an essential part of Derbyshire's batting and earned his county cap. He went from strength to strength and headed the county's averages in 1996, when he scored 1,590 Championship

runs with a massive 239 top score against Hampshire at Southampton. But life at Derby was unhappy and Chris felt isolated, especially when, in 1997, the Australian county captain, Dean Jones, felt obliged to leave the club. He himself had been hoping to leave for some time and his eventual release by the Midland county was a blessing both for him and for Sussex.

After Sussex's poor season in 1996, after which Alan Wells was not retained as captain, the appointment of Peter Moores as his successor for the following season was only seen as a stop-gap measure. Tony Pigott, then the County's chief executive, was seeking a top-class batsman who would lead the side and Chris Adams seemed an obvious choice. He joined Sussex for the start of the 1998 season on a salary reputed to be the highest on the county circuit. His arrival at Hove immediately began to galvanise the team as he scored two hundreds in the match against Essex at Chelmsford and 170 against Middlesex at Hove, an innings of tremendous power which contained 27 fours. These innings were one of the reasons why spectators began to comment that cricket looked a different game when he was at the crease. The County moved dramatically up the Championship table from 18th to 7th place. The following season also brought rewards for,

*Chris Adams is a powerful cutter, playing here for England v. South Africa at the Oval in 1998.*

while Sussex failed by a whisker to become a member of the new First Division, they won – as Sussex Sharks – the second division of the CGU National Sunday League and were promoted to the First Division.

It was not only at Hove that Chris was finding a new lease of life. He had, for some time, believed that he possessed the qualities of an international cricketer and was overjoyed when he was selected in 1998 for limited-over internationals against South Africa at the Oval and Old Trafford. This did not lead to selection for the Test matches in that season, but at the end of the following season his prowess, particularly as a limited-overs batsman who had scored more than 1,000 runs in the short game and had an average of over 77, was again recognised by England's selectors by his inclusion in the touring party to South Africa in the winter of 1999/2000. He played in all five Test matches, although a perceived weakness outside the off-stump often led to his dismissal for relatively low scores, but he batted well in the limited-over matches before a family illness caused him to return early to England.

Sussex's 2000 season, however, again put him in the spotlight as the County finished bottom in both competitions. He accepted fully that the buck stopped with the captain when there was an apparent loss of morale in the team towards the end of the season, one reason being that Michael Bevan had been recalled to play for Australia. Chris's own determination to do well and to put the previous season behind him, together with the establishment of a marvellous opening partnership between Richard Montgomerie and Murray Goodwin, led to a magnificent Sussex revival in 2001. Although they just managed to miss promotion in the limited-overs National League, they won the Second Division Championship and will play in the First Division in 2002. Sussex *aficionados* may choose to argue that this achievement marks the County's first championship, although many will be happy only when the First Division pennant hangs above the pavilion at Hove. After missing some matches owing to injury at the start of the 2001 season, Chris returned to the scene in dramatic fashion, scoring a magnificent 192 against Derbyshire at Arundel and notching two further hundreds. A first-class performance of over 1,000 runs at an average of nearly 52 was a good achievement, but what must have pleased and perhaps surprised him even more was that his 10 wickets at just over 11 runs each meant that he headed the national bowling averages!

# C.W.J. (Bill) Athey
*RHB & RM, 1993-97*

**Born:** Middlesbrough, 27 September 1957

**County Cap:** 1993

**Batting Record:**

| M | I | NO | Runs | Avge |
|---|---|---|---|---|
| 80 | 145 | 9 | 5,324 | 39.15 |
| *79* | *76* | *7* | *2,240* | *32.46* |
| **100** | **50** | | **CT/ST** | |
| 13 | 27 | | 60 | |
| *3* | *14* | | *15/1* | |

**Bowling Record:**

| O | M | Runs | W | Avge |
|---|---|---|---|---|
| 82 | 9 | 334 | 3 | 111.33 |
| *38.5* | *0* | *214* | *6* | *34.00* |
| **5wI** | **10wM** | | | |
| - | - | | | |
| *1* | *-* | | | |

**Career Best Performances:**
169* v. Kent, Tunbridge Wells 1994
10-1-40-2 v. Nottinghamshire, Eastbourne, 1993
*118 v. Kent, Hove, 1995 (B&H)*
*4.2-0-24-2 v. Somerset, Taunton, 1993 (SL)*

The restraint of trade legislation has certainly benefited rolling stones like Bill Athey. Beginning his career with Yorkshire, he was hailed as a top opening batsman, a new Hutton or Boycott. Sadly, he disappointed over eight seasons by passing 1,000 runs only twice in Championship matches and, feeling unhappy, he joined Gloucestershire for the 1984 season. This seemed to do the trick; for in his first season there he moved close to 2,000 runs and scored well for another four seasons. He made over 1,000 runs in 1988 at an average of nearly 75, and was appointed captain for the 1989 season. This did not work and, following a poor season, he relinquished the post after just one year.

He continued for a further three seasons 'in the ranks' and then at the end of 1992 he refused a new contract. Gloucestershire were amazed that Bill, with over 11,000 runs including 28 hundreds for them, would not stay. While in the West Country, he had also represented England in Tests and one-day internationals, scoring a one-day 142 not out against New Zealand in 1986 and forming an excellent opening partnership with Chris Broad on the 1986/87 tour of Australia. He capped these successes with 123 in the Lord's Test against Pakistan in 1987.

He joined Sussex in 1993, by now the finished article as a cricketer. The County needed an experienced opener to bolster the middle order and he filled the bill exactly. Big hundreds, such as his 169 not out against Kent and his 163 against Durham in 1994, together with his 163 not out against Gloucestershire in 1995, were precisely what the County needed. From 1993 to 1996, he scored over 1,000 runs in every season bar one, but then in 1997 he decided to up sticks in August and become Worcestershire's coach. Bill was a talented player who knew how to make the most of his periods of good form, and he was of immense value to a side where the batting could be fragile. Not only did he perform well in the first-class game, but his performance in the short game was mostly valuable, either opening the innings and keeping one end going or coming in to bolster the middle with a solid 50 not out. Occasionally, however, his stubborn streak would show through. Chasing a Shropshire total of 116, Bill was 18 not out from Sussex's 119 for 0 wicket after he failed to score a run between the 23rd and 44th overs!

11

# John R.T. Barclay
*RHB & OB, 1970-86*

| Born: Bonn, Germany, 22 January 1954 | | | | |
|---|---|---|---|---|
| **County Cap:** 1976 | | | | |
| **County Captain:** 1981-1986 | | | | |
| **Batting Record:** | | | | |
| **M** | **I** | **NO** | **Runs** | **Avge** |
| 265 | 422 | 43 | 9419 | 24.55 |
| *232* | *168* | *41* | *2696* | *21.23* |
| **100** | **50** | | **CT/ST** | |
| 9 | 45 | | 211 | |
| - | *6* | | *79* | |
| **Bowling Record:** | | | | |
| **O** | **M** | **Runs** | **W** | **Avge** |
| 3328 | 789 | 9,535 | 312 | 30.56 |
| *991.1* | *79* | *4,135* | *166* | *24.91* |
| **5wI** | **10wM** | | | |
| 9 | 1 | | | |
| - | - | | | |

**Career Best Performances:**
119 v. Leicestershire, Hove, 1980
23.4-6-61-6 v. Sri Lanka, Hove, 1979
*93* v. Surrey, Oval, 1976 (B&H)*
*10.4-2-43-5 v. Combined Universities,*
*Oxford, 1979 (B&H)*

John Barclay was born in Bonn, but his parents moved back to Britain when he was two. They lived in Horsham, close to the cricket ground – the game was in his blood at an early age. At Eton, he was selected for the First XI when only fourteen and he was noted as a promising all-rounder. In 1970, when he actually played two games for Sussex at the age of sixteen, he scored a record 897 runs for his school and took 28 wickets as well. His personality and potential for leadership, together with his cricketing skill, made him an automatic choice for many young cricketers' sides and he captained England Young Cricketers in the West Indies in 1972.

He became a Sussex regular in 1975 and in the next year made exactly 1,000 runs as an opener and, with 30 wickets at 22 each, topped the bowling averages. He was a staple member of the Sussex team for the rest of the 1970s, sometimes reaching 1,000 runs, but usually just missing this target, and he collected a fair tally of wickets, his best return being 52 in 1979. When Arnold Long resigned the captaincy at the end of 1980, John was asked to succeed him.

His first season brought immediate success. The County finished second in the Championship, tantalisingly just two points behind Nottinghamshire, but it was the best result since David Sheppard's year as captain in 1953. In the following year the John Player Sunday League title was won and, apart from the 1983 and 1986 seasons, in the second of which a damaged finger led to his playing in only two matches and retiring thereafter, Sussex were consistently in the top half of the Championship. After his first successful year, *Wisden* noted: 'He displayed sufficient qualities of leadership and enthusiasm for the game to suggest that he could be a future England skipper.' This was perhaps a pious hope; he was an outstanding captain and could always be considered in county cricket an all-rounder in the Mike Brearley style of captain/batsman, but as time went on his personal form declined and Test cricket was surely beyond him.

In 1986 he handed over the reins to Ian Gould, who had led the side in the County's NatWest Cup triumph in that year, yet his tenure as captain had given Sussex as successful a period as any in its recent history.

# Hugh T. Bartlett *DFC*

*LHB & RM, 1937-49*

**Born:** Balaghat, India, 7 October 1914
**Died:** Hove, 26 June 1988

**County Cap:** 1938
**County Captain:** 1947-49

**Batting Record:**

| M | I | NO | Runs | Avge |
|---|---|----|------|------|
| 152 | 247 | 24 | 7,074 | 31.72 |
| 100 | 50 | | CT/ST | |
| 9 | 44 | | 52 | |

**Bowling Record:**

| O | M | Runs | W | Avge |
|---|---|------|---|------|
| 38 | 3 | 187 | 7 | 26.71 |
| 5wI | 10wM | | | |
| - | - | | | |

**Career Best Performances:**
157 v. Australians, Hove, 1938
1-1-0-1 v. Nottinghamshire, Hastings, 1949

In 1933, Hugh Bartlett was described thus: 'The finest left-handed schoolboy batsman of the century'. In three seasons at Dulwich College he scored 2,783 runs with an average above 50, including a remarkable 228 v. Mill Hill with 8 sixes, 2 fives and 25 fours. A Cambridge blue for three years, he first played for Sussex in 1937. In the following season, one in which he hit 40 sixes, his impact was enormous. His 175 not out, made in under three hours with 4 sixes and 24 fours, for the Gentlemen versus the Players, was the second highest innings in this series since C.B. Fry's 232 not out in 1903. A month later, he slaughtered the powerful Australians at Hove with an innings of 157, including 6 sixes and 18 fours, which won him the Lawrence Trophy for the fastest (57 minutes) century of the season.

Hugh was hailed as another Frank Woolley, the best prospect for England's middle batting for a long time, another Jessop, perhaps even a Test captain, but England's batting was strong at this time and he was not picked for any Tests. He was, however, selected for the 1938/39 MCC tour to South Africa, but again failed to make the Test side, although *Wisden* suggested that half an hour of his batting might have finished the timeless Fifth Test at Durban!

The Second World War intervened and Hugh served with distinction in the Glider Pilot Regiment. He became a Major, served at Arnhem and was awarded the DFC. In 1946, he resumed his career with Sussex, but some of the magic seemed to have deserted him. Although he held the captaincy of the County from 1947 to 1949, a not particularly strong side made it a hard task and the committee ousted him in 1950. He retired immediately. His brilliance was pre-war: in the three seasons before 1939, he had an average of nearly 44; in the four seasons after it, his average had dropped to not quite 27. He was perhaps a nervous player: it is said that, if the first ball of an innings passed the bat, he muttered 'Crikey' and put on his pads. Apocryphal perhaps, but what is not is that he could be padded up when batting at number six while the opening pair were still together.

His sad departure from Sussex was rectified in 1977 when he was elected president. He collapsed and died in 1988 while watching Sussex in a Sunday League match, a form of cricket at which he would surely have excelled.

# Donald L. Bates
*RHB & RMF, 1950-71*

**Born:** Hove, 10 May 1933

**County Cap:** 1957

**Batting Record:**

| M | I | NO | Runs | Avge |
|---|---|----|------|------|
| 315 | 358 | 157 | 1,525 | 7.58 |
| *45* | *25* | *13* | *74* | *6.16* |
| **100** | **50** | | **CT/ST** | |
| - | - | | 118 | |
| - | - | | *13* | |

**Bowling Record:**

| O | M | Runs | W | Avge |
|---|---|------|---|------|
| 8400 | 1948 | 22,776 | 880 | 25.88 |
| *400.4* | *49* | *1,474* | *61* | *24.16* |
| **5wI** | **10wM** | | | |
| 34 | 2 | | | |
| *1* | - | | | |

**Career Best Performances:**
37* v. Kent, Tunbridge Wells, 1960
*38 v. Somerset, Torquay, 1969 (SL)*
29.3-10-51-8 v. Essex, Hove, 1966
*12-2-30-6 v. Gloucestershire, Hove, 1968 (GC)*

Don Bates was born a mile from the County Ground in Eaton Road, about two miles from the Goldstone Ground, the former home of Brighton and Hove Albion FC – he is a Sussex man through and through. The son of a school sports master, as a boy he represented Sussex at football, cricket and athletics, Brighton at boxing and Hove Grammar School at swimming. He was a considerable sporting all-rounder and he progressed from Brighton junior soccer to a professional with Brighton and Hove Albion and from Sussex Young Amateurs to a professional with Sussex CCC.

He joined the County staff in 1949 and made his debut in 1950, after which he had to undergo two years' National Service. It was, therefore, not until seven years later that he started to make his mark on the cricket field. In 1957, he took 82 wickets and, although doing rather less well in the next two seasons, he produced excellent form in the first three years of the sixties when he took over 100 wickets in each year. His county captain, Ted Dexter, has described him as an 'old-fashioned bowler', not with any disrespect, but rather the contrary. He saw Don as the sort of medium-fast bowler who, while lacking the pace of the really quick men, pitched the ball up, gave it a chance to swing and committed the batsman to a stroke. There was nothing of the nagging, short-of-a-length bowling on middle-and-leg so often associated with bowlers of his pace. Bounce, too, was his strong point. Not bouncers – his pace did not really allow these – but that extra lift which comes from delivering the ball from one's full height. With the advent of limited-overs cricket he was also a force to be reckoned with, and was a valuable member of the side in the first two years of the Gillette Cup when Sussex twice won the trophy. Don was not a great batsman – in 1957 in consecutive innings he scored 0*, 0, 1, 0, 0*, 1, 0*, 0, 0* and 0*. Indeed, one colleague has described him humorously as the 'photograph' batsman, as he looked excellent in his pose, but was rarely near the ball!

He was a talented right-half in soccer and was in the Brighton and Hove side which gained promotion to the Second Division in 1957/58, but the clash between seasons meant that, in the end, soccer came second to cricket.

# George Bean

*RHB & RM, 1886-98*

**Born:** Sutton-in-Ashfield, Nottinghamshire, 7 March 1863
**Died:** Mansfield, 16 March 1923

**Batting Record:**

| M | I | NO | Runs | Avge |
|---|---|----|------|------|
| 202 | 365 | 15 | 7,326 | 20.93 |
| **100** | **50** | | **CT/ST** | |
| 9 | 32 | | 119 | |

**Bowling Record:**

| O | M | Runs | W | Avge |
|---|---|------|---|------|
| 3,332 | 1,271 | 6,356 | 232 | 27.39 |
| **5wI** | **10wM** | | | |
| 9 | 2 | | | |

**Career Best Performances:**
186 v. Lancashire, Old Trafford, 1893
21.3-8-29-8 v. MCC, Lord's, 1889

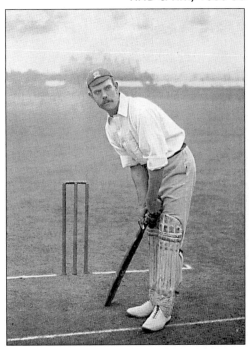

George Bean was one of a number of Nottinghamshire players whom the county released towards the end of the nineteenth century to seek a career elsewhere. He was a hard-hitting batsman, a medium-pace round-arm bowler and a good fielder, especially at cover point. By trade a framework knitter, he opted for cricket in 1882 when he became a professional with the Nottinghamshire Commercial Club and in 1885 he played for the county itself. In the following year, he declined Nottinghamshire's terms and came to Sussex for whom he had qualified by residence, having lived near Sheffield Park since 1884.

From 1886 to 1898, he was an important member of the Sussex team and he made his runs on a Hove wicket that favoured batsmen. It is said that it suited his style to perfection; he had a brilliant cut shot and, as the boundary on the pavilion side was so short, he scored many runs without actually running a yard. In 1891, playing against his native county at Hove, he carried his bat for 145 in the first innings and followed with 92 in the second, while in 1893 he was involved with William Murdoch in a second-wicket partnership of 226 against Lancashire. His bowling also had its successes as he took 8 wickets in an innings on two occasions – for 29 versus MCC at Lord's in 1889 and for 31 versus Yorkshire at Dewsbury in 1891.

In 1891, he was at the height of his powers, heading the Sussex batting averages and ranking among the very best of professional batsmen. As a result he was selected for Lord Sheffield's team which toured Australia in 1891/92 under Dr W.G. Grace's captaincy. England lost the three-match series by two matches to one, but in the first of his three Tests, George scored 50 at Melbourne. The tour seemed to affect his form and 1892 proved a poor season for him, but he recovered in the following season and again led the Sussex batting. Having coached the East London Club in South Africa in 1896/97, he played for two more seasons before retiring in 1898 after a benefit match against Surrey. In 1890 he had joined the Lord's groundstaff, and in his retirement he coached at Haileybury College and umpired from time to time for Sussex. He enjoyed a further benefit in the Middlesex-Sussex match at Lord's in 1921 and, at the time of his death in 1923, he was the senior member of the Lord's staff.

# Michael G. Bevan
*LHB & SLA, 1998 & 2000*

**Born:** Belconnen, Australian Capital Territory, 8 May 1970

**County Cap:** 1998

**Batting Record:**

| M | I | NO | Runs | Avge |
|---|---|----|------|------|
| 24 | 37 | 5 | 2,059 | 64.34 |
| *32* | *31* | *13* | *1,612* | *89.55* |
| 100 | 50 | | CT/ST | |
| 8 | 5 | | 14 | |
| *1* | *17* | | *18* | |

**Bowling Record:**

| O | M | Runs | W | Avge |
|---|---|------|---|------|
| 279 | 38 | 1053 | 24 | 43.88 |
| *66.2* | *1* | *356* | *16* | *22.25* |

**Career Best Performances:**
174 v. Middlesex, Southgate, 2000
13-3-36-3 v. Kent, Tunbridge Wells, 1998
*157* v. Essex, Chelmsford, 2000 (B&H)*
*4-1-7-3 v. Durham, Eastbourne, 1998 (SL)*

No less an authority than Richie Benaud has described Michael Bevan as 'the best one-day batsman in the world'. His performances for Australia's one-day squad have been phenomenal, although he has not been able to clinch a permanent place in his country's Test team. Although he has played for Australia in eighteen Test matches between 1994 and 1998, an apparent weakness outside the off stump appears to have been his undoing.

Michael was born in the Australian Capital Territory and at the age of nineteen made his debut for South Australia, but in 1990 he joined New South Wales. In the 1990/91 season, he scored four successive Sheffield Shield hundreds and, in the course of forty-two days, amassed five hundreds – a feat not surpassed by any Australian except Sir Donald Bradman.

In the 1995 and 1996 seasons, he sampled county cricket with Yorkshire and first came to Sussex in 1998. A predictable scourge of county attacks, he scored 935 runs (average 55.00) and three hundreds, together with over 500 runs in one-day matches. Unable to play in England in 1999, he returned in 2000 to produce the most incredible run of form. Although the season in itself proved a disaster for Sussex, Michael's rich vein of form secured him a place in the record books. Finishing top of the national batting averages with 1,124 runs (average 74.93), he almost equalled Ranji and C.B. Fry who between 1899 and 1905 secured higher seasonal batting averages at a time when fielding standards were arguably not what they are today. Typical of his performances were his 173 not out of 270 for 3 wickets against Middlesex in a match that Sussex, but for his contribution, might have lost and his 166 followed by 174 against Nottinghamshire.

It was a similar story in the one-day format – Michael was completely unstoppable. In the these matches he put together 1,059 runs in 17 innings at an average of 132.37, making a total of 2,183 runs in all competitions. When he had to return to Australia at the end of July, Sussex's season went into reverse and four of the remaining five matches were lost.

He did not play for Sussex in 2001 and he has now become captain of New South Wales. His brilliant limited-overs batting for Australia in 2001/02 augurs well for his new county, Leicestershire, in 2002.

# Cyril G. Bland

*RHB & RF, 1897-1904*

**Born:** Leake, Lincolnshire, 23 May 1872
**Died:** Cowbridge, Lincolnshire, 1 July 1950

**Batting Record:**

| M | I | NO | Runs | Avge |
|---|---|----|------|------|
| 145 | 188 | 35 | 991 | 6.48 |
| 100 | 50 | | CT/ST | |
| - | 1 | | 79 | |

**Bowling Record:**

| O | M | Runs | W | Avge |
|---|---|------|---|------|
| 5,075 | 1,336 | 13,388 | 553 | 24.20 |
| 5wI | 10wM | | | |
| 44 | 11 | | | |

**Career Best Performances:**
59 v. Surrey, The Oval, 1900
25.2-0-48-10 v. Kent, Tonbridge, 1899

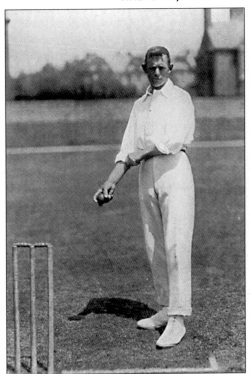

For sixty-five years, Cyril Bland was the holder of an exceptional Sussex record, namely, that of the only bowler to take ten wickets in an innings. Not until 1964 did Ian Thomson equal it. Cyril started his cricketing career in Skegness in his native Lincolnshire, but soon moved into Yorkshire club cricket. After this period he moved to the south, playing club cricket in Hertfordshire and also in Horsham, before qualifying for Sussex for the 1897 season.

His first year with the County, in terms of statistics, was by far his best. He ended with 129 wickets in all matches at an average of 21.60. In the match against Cambridge University he took 14 wickets and bowled unchanged throughout the match with Fred Tate, the first occasion that a Sussex pair had done so for twenty-two years. *Wisden* was kind enough to note: 'Considering he had never gone through the strain of a long season on hard wickets, his success in the Sussex eleven was, to our thinking, one of the chief features of the season of 1897.' Although he bowled very fast, but occasionally erratically, in the next three seasons and passed 100 wickets again in 1899, 395 of his 553 wickets for Sussex were taken in these first four seasons. The match against Kent at Tonbridge in 1899 was, of course, his outstanding performance – in the course of 25.2 allegedly furious overs, he accounted for such eminent scalps as J.R. Mason and A. Hearne.

After 1900, his returns were moderate indeed. In 1904, he left Sussex and apparently gave up the game altogether. What caused this to happen is not clear; it is true that he had been warned by Lord's about the fairness of his action and it is said that, having become friendly with Ranjitsinhji, he had attended a number of 'gentlemen's' parties – he himself, of course, was essentially a young man from the fen country – and he learned to imbibe a little too liberally.

In the First World War, he served with the Veterinary Corps and was slightly wounded, but then he appears to have returned to a rural life in Lincolnshire. What is fairly certain is that, as time went by, he drank too much and suffered increasingly from depression. His death in 1950 was almost certainly suicide, as he was found drowned in a canal at Cowbridge, near Boston.

# Edward H. (Ted) Bowley

*RHB & LB, 1912-34*

**Born:** Leatherhead, Surrey, 6 June 1890
**Died:** Winchester, 9 July 1974

**Batting Record:**

| M | I | NO | Runs | Avge |
|---|---|----|------|------|
| 458 | 773 | 40 | 25,439 | 34.70 |
| **100** | **50** | | **CT/ST** | |
| 46 | 136 | | 324 | |

**Bowling Record:**

| O | M | Runs | W | Avge |
|---|---|------|---|------|
| 6,140 | 1,197 | 17,137 | 667 | 25.69 |
| **5wl** | **10wl** | | | |
| 26 | 2 | | | |

**Career Best Performances:**
283 v. Middlesex, Hove, 1933
39.4-8-114-9 v. Derbyshire, Hove, 1929

Perhaps the equal of Joe Vine and exceeded only by John Langridge, Ted Bowley ranks among the greatest of Sussex's professional batsmen. Although he was born in Surrey, he learned much of his early cricket with his father in Hampshire in the small town of Liss, where it is said that the Sussex-Hampshire border passed through their house. He qualified for Sussex by residence, was coached by Joe Vine and Albert Relf and first played for the County in 1912, establishing himself as a regular member of the side in 1914. In that year he scored 1,000 runs for the first time, including 10 fifties and then, like so many others, served in the Army and did not rejoin the County until 1920. From then until his last full season in 1933, he scored 1,000 runs in each year, his best being 2,354 (average 45.26) in 1928. He was also an excellent right-arm leg-spin bowler who deceived many a high class batsman with his deceptive flight. Unusually, he bowled at least a yard behind the crease and was consequently never no-balled in his career. On top of these all-round skills, he was a superb slip fielder, a role which his pupil John Langridge also filled with distinction.

Ted was the rock on which Sussex batting was built in the 1920s. Few of the County's great batsmen can have carried such a heavy burden as he played in an era when the County's batting

was generally unreliable. In many respects he was, by both technique and inclination, an ideal number four batsman, but the exigencies of the time made him adapt and convert himself into an opener. R.C. Robertson-Glasgow, a correspondent and cricketer himself, saw him as one of the finest back-foot players of the time. He wrote: 'I never saw a batsman who played this stroke with his bat and his elbow so high, meeting a rising ball, which others would leave, with tremendous force, and hammering it straight or to the off-side boundary. Again, he would lean back and cut square from the off stump balls which others were content to stop.' Because he was also so quick on his feet, he was able to drive powerfully off the front foot and he played slow bowlers just as well as the quick men.

He took part in 14 partnerships of over 200 for the County. Two remain County records today: in 1921, Ted (228) and Maurice Tate (203) added 385 for the second wicket against Northamptonshire at Hove, and in 1933 he joined John Langridge (195) in a partnership of 490 for the first wicket against Middlesex, also at Hove, when he scored 283, the highest score ever by a Sussex professional. This partnership remains the fourth highest opening stand in the history of the game. Four years earlier, he had partnered Jim Parks (110) in a similarly large – and at the time record-breaking – opening part-

*Ted Bowley (right) opens England's innings with Herbert Sutcliffe v. South Africa at Headingley in 1929.*

nership of 368 against Gloucestershire, when he went on to make 280 not out.

Representative honours were hard to find at this time in English cricket. Jack Hobbs and Herbert Sutcliffe were regularly at the top of England's batting order and, in their absence, he always had to contend with the likes of Andrew Sandham and Percy Holmes. Ted, who in another era might have played fifty or more times for England, managed only five Tests, two against South Africa in 1929, and a further three against New Zealand in 1929/30 under the leadership of his County captain-elect, Harold Gilligan. At Auckland he scored 109, his only Test hundred. He was, of course, familiar with New Zealand, for he had spent three seasons there as a coach in the 1920s at a time when few

English professionals went abroad for the winter. On one of these trips to New Zealand, he took responsibility for accompanying the young James Langridge there as part of the latter's recuperation from tuberculosis.

Ted was a quiet, almost diffident man, but friendly and full of magnificent advice to younger Sussex batsmen. Jim Parks senior subsequently related: 'Ted set us a marvellous example and it was an education to bat with him. In my view he was the finest professional batsman to play for Sussex.' When he retired at the end of the 1934 season, he carried on this good work for a further twenty-three years at Winchester College, where successive generations of boys profited from his skill, courtesy and friendship.

# Thomas Box
*RHB & WK, 1826-56*

**Born:** Ardingly, 7 February 1808
**Died:** Prince's Cricket Ground, Chelsea, 12 July 1876

**Batting Record:**

| M | I | NO | Runs | Avge |
|---|---|----|------|------|
| 122 | 229 | 27 | 2,671 | 13.22 |
| **50** | **100** | | **CT/ST** | |
| 8 | - | | 125/65 | |

**Bowling Record:**

| Runs | W | Avge |
|------|---|------|
| 66 | 5 | 13.20 |
| **5wI** | **10wM** | |
| 1 | - | |

**Career Best Performances:**
79 v. MCC, Lord's, 1846
5-45 v. England, Brunswick Ground, Hove, 1849

Tom Box played much of his cricket before Sussex became established as a county cricket club. He made his debut in 1826 and played for the County for thirty-one years, not missing a single match in twenty-four of these years. In 1851 he played in no fewer than 43 important matches, an outstanding feat in those days. An unattributed notice remarked: 'Highly gifted as he was by nature, the keeping wicket to such men as Old Lilly and Jem Broadbridge perfected his talent and he was for many years unapproached by anyone but Wenman.' (E.G. Wenman of Kent 1803-79).

Tom was a cabinet-maker by trade, but his life was largely bound up with cricket. He must have been a handsome man because he was known as 'The Adonis of the Cricket Field' until, apparently, he failed to gather a ball which broke his nose! At this time, of course, 'keepers did not wear pads or gloves. For a time, he was ground superintendent at the Prince's Ground, later known as Ireland's Gardens, and he also had a licence for the Royal Gardens and Cricket Ground in the Lewes Road. For five years between 1858 and 1863, after the failure of his cricket outfitters' business, he undertook the management of the Brunswick Ground, 'the cricket ground by the sea', as it was called, situated between Third and Fourth Avenue, Hove. He also became involved in the licensed trade, firstly at the Hanover Arms, then at the Egremont Hotel in Western Road and finally at the Brunswick Hotel, which he ran in conjunction with the Brunswick Ground until 1863. At this point he moved to London to the King's Head in Bear Street, near Leicester Square, which he opened as a meeting place for cricketers. In 1876, while he was altering the scoreboard at a match at the Prince's Ground, he collapsed and died. He was buried in Brompton Cemetery.

In the picture above, with the South Downs in the background, he is standing close to the stumps, with large watchful eyes, curly side whiskers, a white topper (as was usual in those days) and a white shirt with double cuffs. His footwear appears to be sandals! One should perhaps notice that he is standing with his right foot well outside the off-stump. It was usual, apparently, for good class 'keepers to look after the off-side balls and to disregard those on the leg side which the long stop would deal with.

# George Brann

*RHB & RF, 1883-1905*

**Born:** Eastbourne, 23 April 1865
**Died:** Surbiton Hill, Surrey, 14 June 1954

**Batting Record:**

| M | I | NO | Runs | Avge |
|---|---|----|------|------|
| 271 | 447 | 38 | 10,858 | 26.54 |
| **100** | **50** | | **CT/ST** | |
| 24 | 42 | | 135/2 | |

**Bowling Record**

| O | M | Runs | W | Avge |
|---|---|------|---|------|
| 1,092 | 306 | 2,963 | 67 | 44.22 |
| **5wI** | **10wM** | | | |
| 1 | - | | | |

**Career Best Performances:**
161 v. Cambridge University, Hove, 1891
19.2-6-73-5 v. Surrey, Oval, 1899

George Brann was noted as a free-hitting batsman, something of a slogger even in his early days, a quickish bowler and an energetic fielder. A prodigious batsman in his school days at Ardingly College, he once recorded 200 in a house match and scores of over 170 against MCC and Brighton Teachers. He was also a remarkable school athlete, becoming Victor Ludorum for three years and throwing the cricket ball over 115 yards in 1882. He always asserted that he owed much of his cricketing ability to the coaching of Alfred Shaw, the Nottinghamshire and England cricketer, who played and coached for Sussex towards the end of his career. Before he became really involved with the County, George often played club cricket for Ardingly School sides, once scoring 210 against the Brighton Brunswick club. For a short while he taught at his old school before becoming a private tutor, which presumably allowed him more time for sport.

He first played for the County in 1883 and became a mainstay of the County's batting in the 1880s and 1890s before the heady days of Fry and Ranji. Although his best innings for Sussex was 161, he reached 219 in a match against Hampshire in 1886 that was deemed not to be first-class, while in 1892 against Kent he scored two hundreds in a match. Only W.G. Grace (on three occasions) and

W. Lambert for Sussex had previously accomplished this feat. Brann enjoyed touring and went to Australia in 1887/88 under Shaw and Shrewsbury, visited South Africa in 1891/92 in W.W. Read's team and America in 1899 when Ranji was captain. Towards the end of his career he was involved in an 8th wicket partnership with future Sussex captain, C.L.A. Smith, of 229 against Kent at Hove in 1902 – a record that survives today.

George's melancholy, weeping-willow style of moustache belied the cheerful demeanour of a man who was not only a good cricketer – he played soccer for the Corinthians and Sussex and represented England against Scotland and Wales in 1886 and against Wales in 1891. Still a fervent Sussex supporter long after he had retired from cricket, he became an avid golfer of some ability and in 1936, more than fifty years after he first played for the County, he took a party of golfers to South Africa and was pleased that transport had improved since his first visit when he had often had to travel by mule!

21

# Antony (Tony) Buss
*RHB & RFM, 1958-74*

**Born:** Brightling, 1 September 1939

**County Cap:** 1963

**Batting Record:**

| M | I | NO | Runs | Avge |
|---|---|----|------|------|
| 304 | 405 | 75 | 4,250 | 12.88 |
| *101* | *72* | *23* | *437* | *8.92* |

| 100 | 50 | | CT/ST | |
|-----|-----|--|-------|--|
| - | 5 | | 129 | |
| - | - | | *25* | |

**Bowling Record:**

| O | M | Runs | W | Avge |
|---|---|------|---|------|
| 8,593 | 1,983 | 23,442 | 938 | 24.99 |
| *887.1* | *114* | *3,053* | *138* | *22.12* |

| 5wI | 10wM |
|-----|------|
| 42 | 3 |
| *1* | - |

**Career best Performances:**
83 v. Northamptonshire, Hove, 1969
*28 v. Somerset, Taunton, 1966 (GC)*
20.5-8-23-8 v. Nottinghamshire, Hove, 1966
*8-0-53-5 v. Kent, Hove, 1970 (SL)*

It was the fate of Tony Buss to bowl in the shadow of two great bowlers, firstly Ian Thomson and then John Snow, but this did not stop him from becoming a most useful performer in his own right. While he was still at Bexhill Grammar School he was spotted by Alan Oakman, who brought him to Hove for coaching and was groomed for first-class cricket from the age of fourteen. When he left school in 1955, he came on to the County staff and was regarded mainly as an off-spin bowler and batsman. He made his debut in 1958, when the spin bowling was mainly in the hands of Robin Marlar, Alan Oakman and Ron Bell, so he converted to fast-medium pace. By 1960, he was bowling well enough to secure over 50 wickets in a season, but there then followed a forced absence while he undertook National Service with the Royal Air Force, although some representative cricket did come his way during that period.

In 1963, his career took off with a vengeance. In that year and the following four seasons he took 515 wickets for the County, passing 100 wickets in a season on three occasions, and his rhythmical approach and leap before delivery became a familiar sight at Sussex matches. His 113 wickets in the 1967 season was the last occasion when a Sussex bowler performed the feat of reaching 100 wickets In 1965 he twice performed the hat-trick: against Cambridge University at Fenner's and against Derbyshire at Hove. He also managed the same feat in a John Player League match against Warwickshire at Hastings in 1973. When limited-overs cricket came on the scene, his economical bowling was an essential part of the Sussex attack. He performed particularly well in 1963 and 1964, when the County won the first two Gillette finals, and again in 1969 when the John Player League began.

Tony always fancied himself as a batsman and became an excellent night-watchman. 'I wasn't a duffer as a batsman,' he is reputed to have said, 'Many times I went in as night-watchman and stayed there next morning.'

Tony took over the vice-captaincy in 1973 and led the County when Tony Greig was on Test duty. When he retired after the 1974 season, he became coach and then manager until 1980, when financial constraints led to his contract not being renewed.

# Michael A. (Mike) Buss

*LHB & LM, 1961-78*

**Born:** Brightling, 24 January 1944

**County Cap:** 1967

**Batting Record:**

| M | I | NO | Runs | Avge |
|---|---|---|---|---|
| 297 | 517 | 47 | 11,286 | 24.01 |
| *188* | *178* | *10* | *3,498* | *20.82* |

| 100 | 50 | CT/ST |
|---|---|---|
| 9 | 56 | 215 |
| *1* | *16* | *66* |

**Bowling Record:**

| O | M | Runs | W | Avge |
|---|---|---|---|---|
| 5,416 | 1,835 | 13,999 | 481 | 29.10 |
| *1,089* | *150* | *3,906* | *158* | *24.72* |

| 5wI | 10wM |
|---|---|
| 16 | - |
| *3* | *-* |

**Career Best Performances:**
159 v. Glamorgan, Swansea, 1967
*121 v. Nottinghamshire, Worksop, 1971 (SL)*
22.1-7-58-7 v. Hampshire, Bournemouth, 1970
*7-1-14-6 v. Lancashire, Hove, 1973 (SL)*

Michael Buss joined the staff in 1961 as a slow left-arm bowler and lower-order batsman. On his debut, with Sussex's score on 24 for 6, seventeen-year-old Michael played a gritty innings of 33 not out and helped the team reach 113. But it was not *Boys' Own* stuff and it took him until 1966 to establish himself fully in the side. When Ken Suttle dropped down the order, Michael was promoted to open the innings. In his first outing he scored 136, his maiden first-class ton, against Cambridge University, and continued in this position for several seasons. In the winter of 1966/67, he was in Finland visiting his fiancée Ann-Catherine, when he received a call from MCC to join the England Under-25 tour of Pakistan. The change from below freezing in Finland to over 100 degrees in Pakistan may perhaps have had something to do with it, but, sadly, he did not distinguish himself and never received another representative chance.

Despite this setback, Michael proved himself in the 1967 season for Sussex. Against Warwickshire at Hove, he added 144 in 95 minutes with Alan Oakman for the first wicket and he went on to score 124 from a total of 217 for 3 wickets. Shortly afterwards, he batted more sedately for four hours ten minutes to register 159 against Glamorgan at Swansea, the highest score of his career. In the same season, he moved from slow bowling to medium pace to relieve discomfort in his back. For the next few seasons he was a force to be reckoned with, an all-rounder who often reached 1,000 runs and took in the region of 50 wickets, and a limited-overs player whose adventurous batting was often the source of successful run-chases. His opening partner, Geoff Greenidge, once commented: 'When he is on song in his devil-may-care role, to watch him is an experience in itself.' In 1971, partnered by Ted Dexter against Nottinghamshire at Worksop, he hit 15 fours and 3 sixes in his 121 and the pair added 165 at 8 runs per over. With 650 runs he was the highest run-scorer nationally in the Sunday League. By the next season, however, his form as an opener suddenly deserted him. Too much limited-overs cricket may have caused him not to play himself in properly and he gave up opening the batting. He continued, however, to bolster the middle order and to bowl his medium pace with considerable success until the time of his retirement in 1978.

# Henry A. (Harry) Butt

*RHB & WK, 1890-1912*

**Born:** Sands End, Fulham, 27 December 1865
**Died:** Hastings, 21 December 1928

**Batting Record:**

| M | I | NO | Runs | Avge |
|---|---|----|------|------|
| 517 | 753 | 217 | 7,049 | 13.15 |

| 100 | 50 | | CT/ST | |
|-----|----|--|-------|--|
| - | 18 | | 905/260 | |

**Bowling Record:**

| O | M | Runs | W | Avge |
|---|---|------|---|------|
| 10 | 1 | 33 | 0 | -- |

**Career Best Performances:**
96 v. Worcestershire, Hove, 1901
Best season 1905: 87 dismissals (ct 69, st 18)

Harry Butt came to Sussex at the age of ten, but did not play cricket until he was twenty-two. A casual visit to the Hastings Club led to the recognition of his natural ability behind the stumps and two years later he was playing for the County. Less than 5ft 7in tall and not much more than ten stone in weight, he had the 'keeper's agile build, and was also a fine athlete and footballer.

Henry Phillips was doubtless a hard act to follow, but Harry was well able to live up to his predecessor's standards. In his first season, he allowed only one bye while Cambridge University scored 703 for 9 wickets at Hove, and in 1905, through four consecutive matches, he conceded only six byes while 1,938 runs were scored. On three occasions he dismissed six batsmen in an innings and in two matches, the first against Somerset at Hove in 1900 and the second against Kent at Tonbridge, when Cyril Bland took all 10 wickets, he made 8 catches. By 1908 he had made his 1,000th dismissal and two years later, when he was

in his twenty-first season with Sussex, he did not miss a match.

Harry was a sound late-order batsman and he featured in two famous last-wicket partnerships with George Cox senior. In 1906, against Hampshire at Chichester, Harry (42) and George (167*) added 113, and in 1908 against Cambridge University at Fenner's they put on 156, which remains a Sussex record. Good enough to be selected for Lord Hawke's side touring South Africa in 1895/96, he played in the Test matches, conceding a mere nine byes in six innings.

In 1912, he retired from the first-class game and umpired until 1928, officiating in five Test matches. He ranked as high as an umpire as he had as a player. His quiet, but firm, demeanour was respected everywhere and his name was a by-word for fairness. In 1900, he received a £900 benefit (quite a sum in those days) from the Yorkshire match, and in 1928 he was lucky enough to receive a second benefit from the Middlesex-Sussex encounter. By now, however, his health was failing and he informed MCC that he would not stand in 1929. The first-class captains, on hearing of his decision in November 1928, asked MCC to write on their behalf expressing their regret. Sadly, he lived only one month more and died in the December of the same year.

# Herbert P. Chaplin

*RHB & RM, 1905-14*

**Born:** Westminster, London, 1 March 1883
**Died:** Deal, Kent, 6 March 1970

**County Captain:** 1910-14

**Batting Record:**

| M | I | NO | Runs | Avge |
|---|---|----|------|------|
| 169 | 280 | 25 | 6,230 | 24.43 |
| 100 | 50 | | CT/ST | |
| 6 | 29 | | 59 | |

**Bowling Record:**

| O | M | Runs | W | Avge |
|---|---|------|---|------|
| 77 | 8 | 370 | 8 | 46.25 |
| 5wI | 10wM | | | |
| - | - | | | |

**Career Best Performances:**
213* v. Nottinghamshire, Hove, 1914
10-2-47-3 v. Nottinghamshire, Hove, 1913

Educated at Harrow, but at that stage of his career not good enough to reach the school's First XI, Herbert Chaplin went on to Sandhurst, served with the Army in India and made stacks of runs for his regiment, the 10th Hussars. First playing for the County while on leave in 1905, he narrowly missed a hundred when he was run out for 96 against Warwickshire, but at this time most of his cricket was for Brighton Brunswick CC and Sussex Second XI. Only in 1910 did he start to play regularly, succeeding C.L.A. Smith as captain.

In the five years of his captaincy, he only once failed to score 1,000 runs in all matches in a season, although it was initially suggested that he was too self-effacing and batted too low in the order. He scored his first hundred in 1910 when he took 172 not out, made in just under three hours and containing 24 fours, off the Hampshire attack at Southampton. This sort of innings was typical of him: Sussex had lost half of their wickets for 117, but eventually reached 418. This led *Wisden* to comment later that it was 'especially to his credit that several of his best innings were played when runs were most needed.' It could be argued that he was only an average captain who, according to the 1915 *Wisden*, 'left himself open to criticism with regard to the management of his bowling, but there was no lack of courage in his leadership. He was always ready to take a sporting chance.'

His last season for Sussex was also his best. He scored 1,158 runs in all matches and he had the satisfaction of seeing the County reach 6th place in the Championship. In the match against Nottinghamshire at Hove, the visitors had amassed 501 for 3 wickets declared, with Joe Hardstaff senior reaching 213 not out. After a relatively indifferent start, Sussex finally came within two runs of their opponents' total, with Herbert reaching exactly the same score as Hardstaff, both innings being their highest scores in first-class cricket.

After the First World War, he did not play again. In 1947, he coached the County, although he was in his sixties, and in the early 1950s he helped Harrow School in the same capacity. The later stages of his life are unclear – he apparently visited New Zealand in the mid-fifties, used the *nom de plume* B.P. Chapman and ran a taxi business in Hove. He was clearly a man of many parts!

# Thomas E.R. (Tommy) Cook

*RHB & RM, 1922-37*

TOM COOK

**Born:** Cuckfield, 5 February 1901
**Died:** Brighton, 15 January 1950

**Batting Record:**

| M | I | NO | Runs | Avge |
|---|---|----|------|------|
| 459 | 729 | 65 | 20,176 | 30.38 |
| **100** | **50** | | **CT/ST** | |
| 32 | 99 | | 169/1 | |

**Bowling Record:**

| O | M | Runs | W | Avge |
|---|---|------|---|------|
| 1,086 | 205 | 2,880 | 80 | 36.00 |
| **5wI** | **10wM** | | | |
| 1 | - | | | |

**Career Best Performances:**
278 v. Hampshire, Hove, 1930
10.5-1-24-5 v. Northamptonshire, Kettering, 1930

Tommy Cook was a hero in several spheres. He won a gallantry member when in the Royal Navy in the First World War, while in the 1920s he was without doubt a Sussex sporting hero. A young man from a modest background, he made his debut in 1922 in cricket for Sussex and in football for Brighton and Hove Albion. His early days in cricket did not compare with his performance in football. A star with Albion, he played for England against Wales in the 1923/24 season and, although this was his only international cap, he continued to do well as a soccer player. Gradually, however, his cricket began to catch up.

In 1926, he scored his first hundred for the County and the next season saw him score nearly 1,500 runs. Three years later, he took 278 with 35 fours off the Hampshire bowlers at Hove. In 1933 and 1934, he excelled at batting, scoring 1,983 runs (average 47.21) in the first season and 2,132 runs (average 54.66 and sixth in the first-class list) in the second. Indeed, he made double hundreds in successive seasons against Worcestershire. Altogether he passed 1,000 runs ten times in

a season and took part in five partnerships of over 200, the most exciting being the unbeaten 226 he made together with 'Jack' Holmes against Leicestershire in 1937. Many pundits believed that he was unlucky not to gain an England cricket cap and join the select band of double soccer/cricket internationals. There is no doubt that he was highly regarded: in 1935, *Wisden* wrote: 'Cook was one of the few batsmen in England who showed a proper conception of the way to play slow bowling. Not many players, when jumping out to drive, so completely got to the pitch of the ball as he did.'

He had coached cricket in South Africa in the late 1920s and in 1937 he decided to try his luck there again and accepted a coaching appointment in Cape Town. During the Second World War, he joined the South African Air Force, but was seriously injured in an aviation accident in 1943. His recovery took a long time and after the war he returned to England to begin a spell as soccer manager at Brighton. Sadly, this was nowhere near as successful as his playing days and he was soon replaced. Separated from his wife, emotionally as well as physically scarred by his accident and unwell, he became clinically depressed and committed suicide a month before his forty-ninth birthday.

# James H. Cornford
*RHB & RFM, 1931-52*

**Born:** Crowborough, 9 December 1911
**Died:** Harare, Zimbabwe, 17 June 1985

**County Cap:** 1933

**Batting Record:**

| M | I | NO | Runs | Avge |
|---|---|----|------|------|
| 330 | 397 | 145 | 1,352 | 5.36 |
| **100** | **50** | | **CT/ST** | |
| - | - | | 132 | |

**Bowling Record:**

| O | M | Runs | W | Avge |
|---|---|------|---|------|
| 10,375 | 2,255 | 26,934 | 1,019 | 26.43 |
| **5wI** | **10wM** | | | |
| 39 | 6 | | | |

**Career Best Performances:**
34 v. Leicestershire, Ashby-de-la-Zouche, 1949
22-5-53-9 v. Northamptonshire, Rushden, 1949

After playing club cricket in his native Crowborough, Jim Cornford was engaged by the County in 1931, but it was not until 1933 that he started to make his mark. In that season he took 88 wickets at 19.77 runs each in all County matches and *Wisden*, in Jim's obituary, expressed what had been thought at the time: 'With an action clearly modelled on Tate's, he bowled fast-medium, swinging the ball away, while at times making it come back quickly off the pitch and in his early seasons he was regarded as possibly a future England bowler.' He did not fulfil all these promises, although throughout the 1930s he continued to bowl 700 or 800 overs a season, to take his fair share of wickets for Sussex – 96 in 1935 was the best – and to fill a useful place in the attack, often opening the bowling with Maurice Tate.

1939 proved to be a poor season for him and the same was true when cricket resumed in 1946 after the Second World War. Yet in 1947 he bounced back with 94 wickets for the County, and in 1949 he reached his best-ever season's total of 97. In that season he went to bed on the Saturday night of a match with Northamptonshire at Rushden with 9 wickets

under his belt, only to see George Cox take the last wicket first thing on the Monday morning when he had the host's 'keeper, Ken Fiddling, caught at the wicket.

By the early 1950s, Ted James and Jim Wood were leading Sussex's opening attack and Jim's own role was diminishing. In 1949, he had started coaching at St George's College in Salisbury, Southern Rhodesia, and at the end of the 1952 season he emigrated there. He became involved in producing some top players in his adopted country, including Paddy Clift, who played for several seasons for Leicestershire. In addition to his coaching, he became known as an expert on the preparation of wickets in Rhodesia and by the time Salisbury had become Harare and Rhodesia was known as Zimbabwe, he worked on the establishment of the wicket at the Police Ground there which was used for a time as the national ground. At the time of his death, he was still responsible for the wickets at St George's College.

An interesting footnote to his first-class career is that it was reckoned that he bowled 63,206 balls without ever conceding a no-ball!

# Walter L. (Tich) Cornford

*RHB & WK, 1921-47*

**Born:** Hurst Green, 25 December 1900
**Died:** Elm Grove, Brighton, 6 February 1964

**Batting Record:**

| M | I | NO | Runs | Avge |
|---|---|---|---|---|
| 484 | 634 | 207 | 6,430 | 15.05 |
| 100 | 50 | | CT/ST | |
| - | 16 | | 651/334 | |

**Bowling Record:**

| O | M | Runs | W | Avge |
|---|---|---|---|---|
| 11 | 1 | 45 | 0 | — |
| 5wI | 10wM | | | |
| - | - | | | |

**Career Best Performances:**
82 v. Yorkshire, Eastbourne, 1928
Best season 1928: 78 dismissals (ct 57 st 21)

Standing little more than five feet tall, Walter Cornford was probably the shortest wicketkeeper to play first-class cricket and so had little chance of avoiding the nickname 'Tich'. He made his first appearance for Sussex in 1921, but at that time the proficient George Street was well-established behind the stumps and it seemed likely that Tich would be the reserve 'keeper for many years. In 1924, however, George was killed in a traffic accident and this sad and unexpected event allowed Tich to take over the regular spot in the Sussex side. He held it until 1939, although in his last two seasons Billy Griffith used to come into the side in August when he was free of teaching duties at Dulwich College.

He was an outstanding 'keeper, standing up to the stumps, even to the fast-medium deliveries of Maurice Tate, his greatest friend, and Arthur Gilligan, his captain. His skill earned them both a number of stumpings. In 1928 he dismissed eight batsmen in the Worcestershire match and in 1929 he enjoyed a particularly successful match at Hastings, stumping Jack Hobbs in both innings on the leg-side off Bert Wensley and taking five catches off Tate. He was no mean batsman either, often weighing in with a fifty in difficult circumstances, and in 1928, when he made his highest innings of 82 against Yorkshire at Eastbourne, he figured in partnerships with James Langridge of 83 and with Duleep of 111 to save the match after the County had been forced to follow on. In 1933, having been to the wicket nine times without losing his wicket, he was dismissed for the first time on 7 June. On that day, he was put in to open the innings against Lancashire at Old Trafford and John Langridge was demoted to number 3 to accommodate him. He was out for 13 and thus had an average at that point of 86. This may, of course, be an apocryphal story – but perhaps not.

In the winter of 1929/30, he was included in the MCC side to tour Australasia under his county captain-elect Harold Gilligan and he kept wicket in the four inaugural Tests against New Zealand. He did well enough on the tour, but in the Fourth Test, however, the fact that extras numbered 57 (31 byes, 16 leg-byes and 10 no-balls) can have given him little pleasure.

Not re-engaged after the Second World War, Tich found a satisfactory second career as a competent and genial coach at Brighton College.

# George (Old George) Cox
*RHB & LM/SLA, 1895-1928*

**Born:** Warnham, 29 November 1873
**Died:** Dorking, Surrey, 23 March 1949

**Batting Record:**

| M | I | NO | Runs | Avge |
|---|---|---|---|---|
| 618 | 953 | 192 | 14,354 | 18.86 |

| 100 | 50 | | CT/ST | |
|---|---|---|---|---|
| 2 | 54 | | 533 | |

**Bowling Record:**

| O | M | Runs | W | Avge |
|---|---|---|---|---|
| 17,483 | 5,018 | 41,334 | 1,810 | 22.83 |

| 5wI | 10wM |
|---|---|
| 110 | 13 |

**Career Best Performances:**
167* v. Hampshire, Chichester, 1906
36.5-17-50-9 v. Warwickshire, Horsham, 1926

Few cricketers have been such loyal servants of Sussex CCC as George Rubens Cox. He first played for the County in 1895 and he gradually developed into a splendid all-rounder: his right-handed batting was steady or free-hitting as the occasion demanded, and his bowling, at first of medium pace, soon became slow left-arm with an easy flowing action. Being a smart catcher close to the wicket also added to his repertoire. His fitness was legendary in his own lifetime – ten mile walks round Horsham were not unknown – and he continued his career into his fifty-fifth year in 1928.

He made a slow start, but from 1903 he was gathering large hauls of wickets, 164 in 1905 being his best and at the time a County record. His batting progressed too; in 1906, he played what *Wisden* described as 'the innings of his life', when he made 167 not out against Hampshire at Chichester, adding 116 for the last wicket with Harry Butt. Two years later, the same pair established what remains a Sussex last-wicket record partnership, when they scored 156 together in 70 minutes against Cambridge University. In 1921, he had an analysis of 6-6-0-5 against Somerset and in 1926, when he was fifty-two, he bowled out Warwickshire twice almost on his own at Horsham, his 'home ground', so close was it to Warnham. This was a remarkable performance by any standards: more than 75 overs, of which 36 were maidens, and 8 wickets in the first innings and 9 in the second – all for 106 runs.

Later on, when he was senior professional under Arthur Gilligan, he was known as the 'Guv'nor' and something of the strict Victorian martinet in his dealings with the young professionals. But he was never resented and remained highly popular, while some saw him as essentially modest and reticent. To Gilligan he was of great value: 'I think I might shift this chap if you let me try' or, as happened once when Lionel Tennyson came in to bat for Hampshire, 'Skipper, let me have a go at him. He doesn't like my bowling' represented the sort of support he gave. Tennyson, in fact, departed lbw in George's first over.

When he retired in 1928, he coached the young professionals, among them his own son, George. Their combined involvement with Sussex as players and coaches meant that father and son, except for the odd break, served the County for nearly ninety years.

# George (Young George) Cox
*RHB & RM, 1931-60*

**Born:** Warnham, 23 August 1911
**Died:** Burgess Hill, 30 March 1985

**Batting Record:**

| M | I | NO | Runs | Avge |
|---|---|----|------|------|
| 448 | 740 | 57 | 22,687 | 33.21 |
| 100 | 50 | | CT/ST | |
| 50 | 93 | | 136 | |

**Bowling Record:**

| O | M | Runs | W | Avge |
|---|---|------|---|------|
| 2,251 | 584 | 5,889 | 191 | 30.83 |
| 5wI | 10wM | | | |
| 3 | - | | | |

**Career Best Performances:**
234* v. Indians, Hove, 1946
35-4-125-6 v. MCC, Hastings, 1946

George Cox junior, the son of George Rubens Cox, the consummate professional, often played as if he were an old-fashioned amateur. Although cricket was his profession, to him it was always a game and one to be enjoyed. Educated at Collyer's School in Horsham, he first played for Sussex in 1931, but took time to settle. In the winter months he excelled as a centre-forward for Arsenal, Fulham and Luton Town.

His early years at Sussex were lean and it was not until 1935 that he made his first hundred, 162 against Hampshire at Southampton. It was only in 1937 that he began to command a regular place in the side; in this season, he was nine short of 1,900 runs in all matches. In the following season, when Yorkshire seemed set to defeat Sussex by an innings, George reached 50 in 28 minutes and 100 out of 114 in an hour and missed the Lawrence Trophy by three minutes. It has been suggested that the Second World War cost him an England place. In 1939, he scored 414 runs in two days, 232 against Northamptonshire at Kettering and, on the next day, 182 against Lancashire at Hove. However, his most exciting innings was almost certainly his 198 in 200 minutes against Yorkshire in the last match before the war.

After the war, runs continued to flow: 234 not out against the Indians in 1946; 205 not out against Glamorgan in 1947 in a 5-wicket win against all odds; 212 not out in 1949 to save a Yorkshire match. His off-driving through the covers, often when the ball was good length rather than half-volley, always gave the bowlers a chance, and it is significant that in only two of his sixteen full seasons was his average better than the thirties. Even though wickets were uncovered in those days, the benchmark of forty was rarely in sight. Quality perhaps, rather than quantity, may well be his final summing up. Although he rarely bowled before the war, he found that his slow medium 'floaters' were often in demand in Sussex's weak post-war attack and in 1949 he took 30 wickets.

He officially retired in 1955, when he became Winchester College's coach, but he found it hard to leave the game he loved. In 1957, at the age of forty-six, he came back to score his fiftieth hundred and he even played again in 1960. After that he became Sussex coach and from 1965 devoted himself to committee work, captaining the Second XI and amusing people with after-dinner speeches.

# Edward R. (Ted) Dexter *CBE*

*RHB & RM, 1957-72*

**Born:** Milan, Italy, 15 May 1935

**County Cap:** 1959
**County Captain:** 1960-1965

**Batting Record:**

| M | I | NO | Runs | Avge |
|---|---|----|------|------|
| 137 | 238 | 22 | 8,827 | 40.86 |
| *42* | *40* | *5* | *1,168* | *33.37* |

| 100 | 50 | | CT/ST | |
|-----|----|--|-------|--|
| 26 | 36 | | 116 | |
| *1* | *8* | | *16* | |

**Bowling Record:**

| O | M | Runs | W | Avge |
|---|---|------|---|------|
| 1,990 | 452 | 5,699 | 218 | 26.14 |
| *95.5* | *7* | *417* | *21* | *19.86* |

| 5wI | 10wM | |
|-----|------|--|
| 6 | 2 | |
| - | - | |

**Career Best Performances:**
203 v. Kent, Hastings, 1968
*115 v. Northamptonshire,*
*Northampton, 1963 (GC)*
18-11-24-7 v. Middlesex, Hove, 1960
*5-3-6-3 v. Warwickshire, Lord's, 1964 (GC)*

Ted Dexter has been a vibrant figure on the English cricket scene since the late 1950s when he was an undergraduate playing for Cambridge University. Some would rate him, after Peter May perhaps, the greatest English batsman to have emerged since the Second World War. A former Sussex captain, C.B. Fry, when speaking of his contemporary, A.C. MacLaren, said: 'Like all great batsmen, he has always attacked the bowling.' This was certainly true of Ted, for few have allowed the bowler to dominate less than he did in his heyday. His 70 against the might of West Indian fast bowling in the 1963 Lord's Test serves as just one example.

Ted became known as 'Lord Edward', a handsome figure with a naturally aristocratic air, but this gave a false impression. Always friendly to his team-mates, he was more shy than arrogant. Educated at Radley College, where his seasonal average was usually over 80, he became part of the Cambridge University team in the 1956 season, gaining a blue in each of his three years, scoring over 1,000 runs in two of them and captaining the side in 1958. He first played for Sussex in 1957, but it was not until 1959 that he took a full part in the County's programme. By the following season he was captain and he led the County for a further five years until 1965. As happens to gifted players, Ted soon found himself picked for his country. While still at Cambridge in 1958, he was called up for the Fourth Test against New Zealand and in the following winter he scored 141 against them at Christchurch. A remarkably successful tour of the West Indies in 1959/60, in which he scored two hundreds, cemented his place in England's ranks and by the time of the eight-Test winter tour of the Indian sub-continent in 1961/62, he had become England's captain and scored 205 in the Third Test at Karachi. He remained captain for a further 22 matches after this tour, including a successful visit to Australia in 1962/63, and his record of 9 wins against 7 losses with 14 matches drawn is not the worst by any means.

It is perhaps inevitable that a successful Test cricketer and captain cannot devote the same amount of time to his county as others less able, but Ted's record for Sussex is uniformly good.

*Ted Dexter, as England captain, introduces his team to HM The Queen and the Duke of Edinburgh in the Second Test v. West Indies at Lord's in 1963.*

The County twice reached fourth place in the Championship under him and only once – in his last season – did they perform less than well. Although he might have tended to over-theorise in the long game, his leadership in the one-day game was exceptional. He understood before anyone else that 60 overs (as the Gillette Cup initially required) was a long time and 'knock-about' tactics were not what this type of game was about. He out-thought other captains by realising that defensive fields, where the opposition was challenged to break through, played an important part. The result was that Sussex lifted the Gillette Cup in its first two years of 1963 and 1964 and a pattern of success for the County in this type of cricket was set.

His own style of batsmanship was ideal for the one-day game, but in the Championship he scored heavily too. It is often forgotten that some great batsmen also bowl: his languid approach to the wicket to bowl his medium pace often belied his ability to break partnerships and in the 1962 season he secured 60 wickets in the Championship. He did not lead England after 1964 and resigned the Sussex captaincy at the end of the 1965 season. He bowed out to try to enter politics, but failed to unseat the future prime minister, James Callaghan, in Cardiff. In 1968, he returned to first-class cricket and in his first innings for Sussex after this break he scored 203 against Kent at Hastings. This led in that year to his recall to the England side for the last two Tests against Australia. Although he played no further first-class cricket after that season, he continued to turn out for Sussex in limited-overs games as late as 1972.

Ted Dexter's versatility is well known. He was a magnificent golfer who might, one supposes, had he been a professional, have played in the Ryder Cup; he flew his own private aircraft to Australia, owned horses and greyhounds, wrote and commentated on cricket and ran a PR company. In 1989, he became chairman of England's selectors, a task for which, apparently, he was excellently qualified, but a mercurial England side and some adverse media attention meant that his spell in charge was relatively unsuccessful. Today an icon in English cricket, he was appointed CBE in 2001 and assumed the MCC presidency for 2001/02.

# Michael J. Di Venuto

*LHB & RM/LB, 1999*

**Born:** Hobart, Tasmania, 12 December 1973

**County Cap:** 1999

**Batting Record:**

| M | I | NO | Runs | Avge |
|---|---|----|------|------|
| 16 | 28 | 2 | 1,067 | 41.03 |
| *18* | *18* | *4* | *772* | *55.14* |
| 100 | 50 | | CT/ST | |
| 3 | 5 | | 20 | |
| - | *8* | | *7* | |

**Bowling Record:**

| O | M | Runs | W | Avge |
|---|---|------|---|------|
| 13 | 2 | 40 | 1 | 40.00 |
| 5wI | 10wM | | | |
| - | - | | | |
| - | - | | | |

**Career Best Performances:**
162 v. Gloucestershire, Hove, 1999
*94* v. Nottinghamshire, Hove, 1999 (SL)*
2-0-3-1 v. Somerset, Taunton, 1999

Michael Di Venuto, 'Diva' in Australian circles, became Sussex's overseas player in the 1999 season owing to Michael Bevan's unavailability. He enjoyed a successful season both in terms of performances and in popularity with both team and members.

He arrived at Hove with a good pedigree including 9 limited-overs international appearances for Australia, captaincy of Australia 'A' sides and steady performances in the Sheffield Shield. His 189 for Tasmania against Western Australia in the Shield final at Perth in a match, albeit one that his side lost, caused commentators to question, according to *Wisden Australia*, whether the national selectors were missing out on a talent 'whose waste would be too tragic to contemplate'. Later, other critics have noted his failure to convert fifties into hundreds and a batsman who, despite being 'a hooker and puller without peer' needed to pay greater attention to shot selection.

In any event, his help in Sussex's 1999 season, one in which they won the Second Division of the National League and were promoted but failed, only by a whisker, to gain First Division Championship status, was invaluable. He was the only Sussex batsman to record over 1,000 runs in Championship matches, but his most enduring memory of Sussex will, however, be his fourth Championship match – that against Gloucestershire at Hove in May. The visitors posted a healthy 294 in their innings to which Sussex replied with a rather paltry 145 and avoided the follow-on by a single run. Batting again, Gloucestershire ran up 302 for 8 wickets before declaring, leaving their hosts a monumental 452 to win. At the close on the third evening, the County had slipped to 127 for 3 wickets and one can imagine that the visitors were calculating at what time they might be setting off for home. Michael was 56 not out overnight and was batting with Tony Cottey. In the course of 73 overs, the two added 256 for the fourth wicket before Michael was dismissed for 162. Sussex, in reaching their target, admittedly with two wickets left, had recorded the second-highest total to win a Championship match. Only Middlesex's 502 for 6 wickets against Nottinghamshire in 1925 exceeded it.

He also made a significant contribution to Sussex's one-day matches, scoring over 700 runs. At the end of the season, there was genuine sadness at Diva's departure. He had been an inspired choice of overseas player and his swashbuckling batting and his affable nature had been a great hit in the county.

# G.H.G. (Hubert) Doggart
*RHB & OB, 1948-61*

**Born:** Earls Court, London, 18 July 1925

**County Cap:** 1949
**County Captain:** 1954

**Batting Record:**

| M | I | NO | Runs | Avge |
|---|---|-----|------|-------|
| 155 | 253 | 17 | 6,716 | 28.45 |
| 100 | 50 | | CT/ST | |
| 13 | 32 | | 157 | |

**Bowling Record:**

| O | M | Runs | W | Avge |
|---|---|------|---|-------|
| 283 | 66 | 826 | 20 | 41.30 |
| 5wI | 10wM | | | |
| - | - | | | |

**Career Best Performances:**
162* v. Cambridge University, Cambridge, 1958
3-0-4-2 v. Nottinghamshire, Trent Bridge, Nottingham, 1954

Hubert Doggart, educated at Winchester College and Cambridge University, made his first-class debut in 1948 for both university and county. He began with 215 not out for Cambridge against Lancashire, the highest score by an Englishman in his first match since 1826. In the following season, partnered by John Dewes and making 219 not out himself, he took part in a stand of 429 against Essex, which at the time was the highest second-wicket partnership in English cricket and only 26 runs short of the world record. In this momentous year, he scored over 2,000 runs. At Cambridge his skill was not confined to cricket; a soccer blue and half-blues in three other sports came his way. For Sussex he was beginning to make his mark too. In 1949, he scored two hundreds, including 155 against Somerset, and it was no surprise that during his captaincy of Cambridge in 1950 he was called into the England side to bat at number four against the West Indies. After two Tests, he was dropped in favour of his record-breaking partner, John Dewes, and not invited ever again. He is not the first cricketer for whom two matches were considered an ample test by England's selectors!

After Cambridge, Hubert went back to Winchester to teach and first-class cricket was, sadly, restricted to the holidays; however, in 1954 he was given leave to take over the captaincy of the County. David Sheppard was a hard act to follow, but Sussex played well under his leadership and some good wins were achieved, especially the double over Worcestershire and the defeat of Middlesex by 8 wickets at Hove in August. His own contribution amounted to over 1,600 runs and he topped the Championship bowling averages, albeit with only 4 wickets!

From 1955 onwards, Hubert was again restricted to matches in the school holidays, but his sound batting, occasional off-spin and brilliant close fielding always gave him a deserved place in the County side. Indeed, in 1958, he recorded 162 not out against his former university and finished in twelfth place in the national averages. He might, however, be likened to men like Arthur Gilligan and Billy Griffith, both of whom gave more to cricket than just that which takes place on the field of play. After becoming headmaster of King's School, Bruton, he served as president of both the MCC and the Cricket Society, and was president of the English Schools Cricket Association for over thirty years.

# Kumar Shri (Duleep) Duleepsinhji
### RHB & LB, 1924-32

**Born:** Sarodar, India, 13 June 1905
**Died:** Bombay, 5 December 1959

**County Captain:** 1931-1932

**Batting Record:**

| M | I | NO | Runs | Avge |
|---|---|---|---|---|
| 119 | 187 | 9 | 9,178 | 51.56 |
| 100 | 50 | | CT/ST | |
| 35 | 31 | | 162 | |

**Bowling Record:**

| O | M | Runs | W | Avge |
|---|---|---|---|---|
| 94 | 4 | 444 | 5 | 88.80 |
| 5wI | 10wM | | | |
| - | - | | | |

**Career Best Performances:**
333 v. Northamptonshire, Hove, 1930 (the highest score recorded by a Sussex batsman)
5-1-21-1 v. Nottinghamshire, Eastbourne, 1929

Kumar Shri Duleepsinhji was one of the most gifted, as well as the most graceful, batsmen ever to represent Sussex. He came to England in 1919 to attend Cheltenham College before moving on to Cambridge University. His uncle, Ranji, had arranged for C.B. Fry to be his guardian during the time of his education and during that period his cricket flourished. At school Duleep, as he inevitably became known, was a prolific batsman and was often among the wickets with his leg-spin bowling. His first-class career began before he left school when he played for MCC, Sussex and the Rest of England in 1924. He went up to Cambridge in the following autumn, won his blue in his first season and enjoyed university cricket for three further seasons. In the vacations he played for Sussex, although illness, which dogged him throughout his life, precluded his playing in 1927.

Having graduated from Cambridge, Duleep returned to India in the winter of 1928/29 and received overtures from the newly-formed Indian Board of Control to throw in his lot with his native country's cricket. It appeared as if the captaincy was his for the taking. At this point Ranji, with his strong affection for all things

English, persuaded his nephew to remain in the game in England. He dutifully returned to this country and began his career with Sussex in 1929. In the match against Kent at Hastings in August, in which 1,451 runs were scored for the loss of 36 wickets, he became the fifth player to record a hundred and a double-hundred in the same game. His 246 in the second innings lasted no more than three-and-a-quarter hours and contained 5 sixes and 31 fours. He ended the season with over 2,000 runs and it was not surprising that he had already attracted the attention of the England selectors. He played his first Test against South Africa, but was dropped after one match. Bitterly disappointed by this treatment, he toyed with leaving the game, but Ranji again stepped in and Duleep was invited to tour Australasia in the winter of 1929/30 under the leadership of his county colleague, Harold Gilligan. He scored nearly 900 runs on the tour, including 368 in the four Tests against New Zealand, so that it was almost a formality that he found himself in the running for the England side in 1930 against Australia. In the Second Test at Lord's, his first against Australia, he scored 173 off a strong attack and ended the series second only to Herbert Sutcliffe in the England batting averages. When he was caught for 173 by Bradman in the outfield from a skyer

*Duleep after scoring 254\* for Cambridge v. Middlesex, 1927.*

off Grimmett, Ranji, from his seat in the pavilion, is alleged to have turned to his neighbour and said: 'The boy was always careless!'

His highest innings in 1930, however, was the 333 which he took off Northamptonshire at Hove in May. Batting for five-and-a-half hours, he hit a six and 35 fours, completed the innings on the first day and eclipsed his uncle's 285 not out against Somerset in 1901. To this day, it has remained the highest innings ever recorded by a Sussex batsman. Ending the season with over 2,500 runs, Duleep had become the County's premier batsman and it was no surprise that he was awarded the captaincy for 1931. It was a season of great success: Sussex moved from seventh to fourth place in the Championship and he scored 1,859 runs at an average of over 58 in this competition and 2,686 overall. He aimed to do better in 1932 and succeeded: Sussex reached second place, but the pressures of leadership were to prove greater than he expected and in the middle of August Duleep's health gave way. He collapsed during Sussex's

game with Somerset at Taunton. The pulmonary tuberculosis that had laid him low five years previously was returning and he was forced to hand over the captaincy to Robert Scott. Had this not been so, Sussex might not still be looking for their first Championship. He decided not to play in the 1933 season and later announced that he was to return to India. He worked at times in cricket administration and in 1949 joined the Indian foreign service, becoming High Commissioner in Australia and New Zealand. On his return, he took on posts in the State of Saurashtra, which he was still holding at the time of his death in 1959 at the age of just fifty-four.

Duleep's career in cricket was, sadly, a short one, but this elegant batsman, unquestionably the best amateur to play between the wars, certainly left his mark on the game. Ronald Aird, quoted in Duleep's obituary in *Wisden,* summed him up well: 'He was not only a very great cricketer, but he also possessed a charming and gentle nature which endeared him to all his many friends.'

# Charles B. Fry
## RHB & RFM, 1894-1908

**Born:** West Croydon, Surrey, 25 April 1872
**Died:** Child's Hill, Hampstead, London, 7 September 1956

**County Captain:** 1904-1908

**Batting Record:**

| M | I | NO | Runs | Avge |
|---|---|----|------|------|
| 236 | 388 | 25 | 20,626 | 56.82 |
| **100** | **50** | | **CT/ST** | |
| 68 | 76 | | 143 | |

**Bowling Record:**

| O | M | Runs | W | Avge |
|---|---|------|---|------|
| 961 | 265 | 2,714 | 86 | 31.55 |
| **5wI** | **10wM** | | | |
| 3 | 1 | | | |

**Career Best Performances:**
244 v. Leicestershire, Leicester, 1901
22.3-8-46-5 v. Worcestershire, Worcester, 1899

Charles Fry is one of the legendary figures of English cricket and he may even be considered the greatest sportsman of all time. He was educated at Repton and Oxford University, where he won twelve blues and captained the University at soccer, athletics and cricket, all in the same year. But he was more than a sportsman: he had won a senior scholarship to Wadham College and gained a First in Classical Moderations. Owing to other distractions, however, largely on the sports field, he achieved only a Fourth in his finals. All sports seemed to come easily to him; he played soccer for England and reached the FA Cup final with Southampton, he equalled the world long-jump record with a leap of over 23ft and, but for injury, would have won an Oxford rugby blue. Cricket was, however, his premier sport.

He joined Sussex in 1894 and large partnerships with Ranji soon became the order of the day – the technically correct Charles contrasted well with Ranji's flashing bat. His scholarly nature had led him to study the technique of batting and this, together with his powers of concentration, allowed him to master most bowlers under most conditions. He had a cast-iron defence and a good straight drive and was particularly apt at working the ball away on the leg-side. When a critic taunted him by saying that he had only one stroke, he replied: 'True, but I can send it to 22 places!' Between 1899 and 1905, he scored 2,000 runs in a season on six occasions and in 1901 he compiled 3,147 runs (average 78.67) with 13 centuries – 6 of them in successive innings. This latter record has never been surpassed and has been equalled only twice – by Sir Donald Bradman and Michael Proctor. In the eight seasons from 1898 to 1905 he was twice first in the English batting averages and four times second. In 1901, he began a fruitful opening partnership with Joe Vine, whom he persuaded to play an anchor role while he himself set about the bowling. Touring abroad clearly did not appeal to him; he never visited Australia and went to South Africa only once – in 1895/96 – when he played the first of his twenty-six Test matches for England. From 1899, he was a something of a fixture in the England side, scoring hundreds against Australia in 1905 and South Africa in 1907. Taken overall, his Test record, if compared to his form in first-class cricket, was unremarkable – a batting average of only 32. After he had moved to Hampshire, he found himself captaining

Left: *Charles Fry autographs the bat with which he scored 6 consecutive centuries in 1901 at his retirement parade from TS* Mercury *in 1950. Right: Charles demonstrates his back-foot play in the nets.*

England in a winning side in the Triangular Tournament with Australia and South Africa in 1912.

His contribution to Sussex cricket was immense. He captained the County from 1904 to 1908, sharing the task with C.L.A. Smith in 1906. His career batting average was 56 and he scored 12 double hundreds, something that only Ranji has bettered, while his 68 centuries have been exceeded only by John Langridge, who played two-and-a-half times as many innings as Charles. In 1898, he married Beatrice Holme Sumner, a lady ten years older than himself, and in 1908 they began a joint venture running the Cadet Training Ship *Mercury* at Hamble, near Southampton. Although it seems that, while he was nominally Captain Superintendent, his wife probably undertook the lion's share of the work. His association with *Mercury* lasted, however, until 1950. As a consequence of this venture, he transferred his cricket allegiance to Hampshire in 1909 – for whom he made his highest score, 258 not out against Gloucestershire in 1911, and for whom he played until 1921 when he was fifty years of age.

Great cricketer that he was, Charles Fry was very much more than that. He wrote several books of lasting value on cricket, a novel in conjunction with his wife and a notable autobiography called *Life Worth Living*. He also edited his own *Fry's Magazine*, and was a columnist for many other journals. An interest in politics led him into friendship with several Liberal and Labour politicians. He made one, albeit unsuccessful, attempt to enter Parliament and he even flirted with fascism, meeting Hitler in 1934 and advising him, presumably as a result of his work on *Mercury*, on how to build up a 'youth movement'. When Ranji was representing India at the League of Nations, Charles joined him in their deliberations in Geneva. Perhaps, however, the most bizarre event in his life occurred in 1921, when he was offered the crown of Albania. Tempted at first by the thought that his great friend Ranji was now the Jam Sahib of Nawanagar, he eventually declined on the grounds that it would be difficult to afford!

Lord Colin Cowdrey praised Charles as 'the greatest athlete and sportsman England ever had.' Few Sussex cricketers, for sure, can have had such an amazing life.

# Arthur E.R. Gilligan
## RHB & RFM, 1920-32

**Born:** Denmark Hill, London, 23 December 1894
**Died:** Mare Hill, Pulborough, 5 September 1976

**County Captain** 1922-1929

**Batting Record:**

| M | I | NO | Runs | Avge |
|---|---|----|------|------|
| 227 | 361 | 30 | 6,712 | 20.27 |
| **100** | **50** | | **CT/ST** | |
| 8 | 20 | | 129 | |

**Bowling Record:**

| O | M | Runs | W | Avge |
|---|---|------|---|------|
| 4,863 | 1,070 | 13,389 | 637 | 21.01 |
| **5wl** | **10wM** | | | |
| 32 | 3 | | | |

**Career Best Performances:**
144 v. Worcestershire, Worcester, 1928
14-5-25-8 v. Middlesex, Lord's, 1924

Arthur Gilligan was one of the real stars in Sussex and English cricket in the 1920s, a fast bowler of panache, a hard-hitting lower-order batsman and a marvellous fielder at mid-off. The middle one of three cricketing brothers, he was educated at Dulwich College and Cambridge University. At school he was an expert athlete as well as a cricketer and just before the First World War he had a few games for Surrey Second XI. He served in the Lancashire Fusiliers during the war and continued with Surrey for a short while afterwards. At Cambridge, he was a force to be reckoned with. In the 1919 Varsity match he took six Oxford wickets with some of the best fast bowling reputedly seen in this match for many years and, when the University played Sussex, he went in last and joined in a stand of 177 in sixty-five minutes, his own share being 101. This was the first of his lightning-fast, lower-order innings, and by the end of his career he had made a hundred batting at numbers 6 to 11 inclusive, something nobody else has achieved.

In 1920, he joined Sussex, for whom he continued to play until 1932, captaining them from 1922 to 1929. In the winter of 1922/23, he

was picked for the MCC tour of South Africa and played in two Test matches. In the following summer, at the height of his powers, he did the double, making over 1,100 runs and taking 163 wickets in all matches. In 1924, when he was picked to lead England in the First Test, he and his county colleague, Maurice Tate, bowled South Africa out for 30 on a flat wicket, his own analysis being 6 wickets for 7. At this particular point in time, the Sussex pair were the most formidable opening bowling combination in the world. A few weeks before the Test, they had bowled out two of the strongest batting sides in England, Surrey for 53 at the Oval and Middlesex for 41 at Lord's, Arthur's share in the latter match being 8 for 25. By the end of June, he had captured 74 wickets at 15 runs each, and, if Arthur's injury had not occurred, Sussex might well have been champions.

Events, however, conspired against him. Playing for the Gentlemen against the Players in the Oval match, he was struck over the heart by a rising ball and was badly hurt. He made light of the injury and continued to play, scoring 112 in the second innings and taking part in a last-wicket partnership of 134. He had, however, underestimated the seriousness of his injury. He was never able to bowl really fast again and, in some respects, was never the same cricketer.

39

*Arthur Gilligan as captain of England in 1924, when he took 6 for 7 and Maurice Tate took 4 for 12 against South Africa. From left to right, back row: R. Kilner, E. Tyldesley, M.W. Tate, A.P.F. Chapman, G.E.C. Wood, C. Parkin, H. Sutcliffe. Front row: E. Hendren, P.G.H. Fender, A.E.R. Gilligan (captain), J.B. Hobbs, F.E. Woolley.*

This, however, did not stop him taking MCC to Australia in the winter of 1924/25 and, while the series was lost 4-1, England's win by an innings in the Fourth Test was their first post-war victory against Australia. His own bowling was very expensive – 10 wickets at 51.90 each – and his highest score was only 31, but many felt that Arthur's inspiring leadership and enthusiasm had helped to restore English cricket to its former position of respect with the Australian public after the debacles of 1920 and 1921.

For Sussex, he displayed the same commitment to success as he had for England. In 1926, his Test career over, but now a selector, he again scored 1,000 runs and he made 4 centuries. In the following winter, he took an MCC side to India, not then a Test-playing country, and brought the side through undefeated. As a captain he may not have been in the front rank of tacticians, but nobody could get more from a team. A strict, but fair, disciplinarian, he would not tolerate slack fielding and his own brilliant

example, especially at mid-off, was an inspiration. But, as his own form tailed off towards the end of the 1920s, his leadership was improving Sussex's cricket, and in his last two years of captaincy they finished in seventh and fifth place respectively in the Championship. After the 1929 season, he relinquished the captaincy and handed over to his brother Harold, but continued to play some matches until 1932.

After he retired from active cricket he moved first into journalism and broadcasting, forming a popular radio partnership with the Australian, Victor Richardson, and writing *Sussex Cricket*, and other books on tours like *The Urn Returns* and *Australian Challenge*.

As time went by, he immersed himself in administration, supporting Sussex and cricket in general, becoming president of both his own county and MCC. E.W. Swanton sums him up well: 'His record as an all-rounder was notable enough, but off the field I judge his endeavours to have been of even greater value to cricket.'

# A.H.H. (Harold) Gilligan AFC
*RHB & LB, 1919-31*

**Born:** Denmark Hill, London, 29 June 1896
**Died:** Shamley Green, Surrey, 5 May 1978

**County Captain:** 1930

**Batting Record:**

| M | I | NO | Runs | Avge |
|---|---|----|------|------|
| 289 | 477 | 30 | 7,829 | 17.51 |
| 100 | 50 | | CT/ST | |
| 1 | 37 | | 111 | |

**Bowling Record:**

| O | M | Runs | W | Avge |
|---|---|------|---|------|
| 1177 | 182 | 3,812 | 114 | 33.43 |
| 5wI | 10wM | | | |
| - | - | | | |

**Career Best Performances:**
143 v. Derbyshire, Hove, 1929
6.1-2-13-4 v. Northamptonshire, Northampton, 1922

Harold Gilligan was always going to be overshadowed by his more famous brother, Arthur, although he, in fact, had a longer stint with the County. The three Gilligan brothers – Frank, the eldest, played for Essex – were educated at Dulwich College and after that Harold and Arthur both moved on to Cambridge, while Frank was at Oxford.

In the First World War, Harold served as an instructor in the Royal Naval Air Service and became the first pilot to fly over the German fleet at Kiel; sadly, his plane developed engine trouble which caused him to spend three days and nights in the North Sea before he was rescued. In 1919, he came into the Sussex side and played continuously for them until 1931 and, having captained them quite often in his brother's absence, he became official captain in 1930.

Harold was never in the same league as his brother, but he was a shrewd captain and a dogged batsman, occasionally opening with Ted Bowley, although he was generally happier hitting hard down the order. His batting career, taken overall, was probably disappointing. A beautiful stylist, he often got out to an impetuous shot and of the 38 times that he passed fifty for Sussex, he converted only one score into a hundred, when he made 143 against Derbyshire at Hove in 1929. He made nearly 8,000 runs for the County, but 3,000 of these runs were scored in the three seasons of 1923, 1927 and 1929, and in the first of these seasons, when he played 70 first-class innings (a record for any one season), he scored 1,186 runs at an average of only 17.70. This average is the lowest for any batsman scoring 1,000 runs in a season.

In the winter of 1929/30, when his brother had to withdraw owing to ill health, Harold was asked to lead an MCC side to Australia and New Zealand. In the early matches in Australia he made 3 fifties against state sides and, later, 70 against Otago in New Zealand. More importantly, he led England to a 1-0 victory in the four-match inaugural series against New Zealand.

Harold Gilligan was a sturdy cricketer, who batted doggedly, fielded brilliantly and, in his early days, bowled some tidy leg-spin. In later years he served on the Surrey Committee and his daughter, Virginia, married the great Surrey and England batsman, Peter May.

# Murray W. Goodwin
*RHB & RM/LB, 2001-*

**Born:** Harare, Zimbabwe, 11 December 1972

**County Cap:** 2001

**Batting Record:**

| M | I | NO | Runs | Avge |
|---|---|----|------|------|
| 17 | 32 | 5 | 1,654 | 61.25 |
| *21* | *21* | *3* | *811* | *45.05* |

| 100 | 50 | | CT/ST | |
|-----|-----|--|-------|--|
| 7 | 5 | | 7 | |
| *1* | *8* | | *5* | |

**Bowling Record:**

| O | M | Runs | W | Avge |
|---|---|------|---|------|
| 11 | 1 | 40 | 0 | -- |

**Career Best Performances:**
203* v. Nottinghamshire, Trent Bridge, 2001
*108 v. Middlesex, Hove 2001 (B&H)*

When Michael Bevan rested from continuous first-class cricket in 2001, Sussex were fortunate to secure the services of Murray Goodwin. Born in Harare, he moved at the age of thirteen with his family to Western Australia and later attended the Australian Cricket Academy. He made his debut for Western Australia in 1994/95, but, unsurprisingly, found it difficult to establish himself in a strong batting line-up. Only in 1996/97 did he start to excel for his state, scoring 127 and 77 against Queensland and ending the season with an average above 61. It was clear that he was unlikely to realise his ambition to play Test cricket in such a competitive country as Australia, so in 1997 he returned to Zimbabwe and immediately attracted their selectors' attention. Making his debut in the series against Sri Lanka and New Zealand in the winter of 1997/98, he twice passed 50, and in the adjoining limited-overs series he made 111 at Colombo.

His cricket went from strength to strength. The Pakistani tour of Zimbabwe in 1998 saw Murray score a massive 166 not out at Bulawayo and lead the batting with an average of exactly 100, while further success followed against India, Pakistan again and finally during the Zimbabwe tour of England in 2000. Here he scored 148 not out at Trent Bridge which, in the words of *Wisden*, 'revealed him as a batsman of true class'. Owing to the disturbances in Zimbabwe, he then decided, sadly, to retire from international cricket.

At the end of 2000, Sussex had lost two openers, leaving only Richard Montgomerie in that role. Murray, although by nature and previous experience a number three, readily took on an opening slot and made it work for him. 94 in his first knock was followed shortly by 195 against Hampshire, 109 against Worcestershire and, at Trent Bridge, 115 in the first innings followed by 203 not out in the second, when he and Richard Montgomerie added 372 without loss before the declaration. Their stand was well short of Ted Bowley's and John Langridge's opening stand of 490 against Middlesex in 1933, but it was the third best for any wicket in the County's history. What he gave to the batting in terms of runs and to the dressing room by way of morale has made him almost indispensable to Sussex cricket, and team and members alike are delighted to know that a two-year contract will keep him at Hove until the end of 2003 at the earliest.

# Ian J. Gould
*LHB & WK, 1981-90*

**Born:** Slough, Buckinghamshire, 19 August 1957

**County Cap:** 1981
**County Captain:** 1987

**Batting Record:**

| M | I | NO | Runs | Avge |
|---|---|----|------|------|
| 195 | 262 | 45 | 6,266 | 28.87 |
| *196* | *179* | *28* | *3,406* | *22.56* |
| **100** | **50** | | **CT/ST** | |
| 3 | 37 | | 346/33 | |
| - | *19* | | *144/11* | |

**Bowling Record:**

| O | M | Runs | W | Avge |
|---|---|------|---|------|
| 75 | 6 | 364 | 8 | 45.50 |
| *3.2* | *0* | *16* | *1* | *16.00* |
| **5wI** | **5wM** | | | |
| - | - | | | |

**Career Best Performances:**
125 v. Hampshire, Hove, 1989
*88 v. Yorkshire, Leeds, l986 (NWT)*
4-1-10-3 v. Surrey, Oval, 1989
*0.2-0-0-1 v. Minor Counties, Hove, 1987 (B&H)*
Best Season: 1984 (67 dismissals, 61 ct, 6 st)

Ian Gould's cricketing career began with Middlesex, for whom he played between 1975 and 1980. Although he played little or no cricket at school he was fortunate enough to qualify for coaching at Lord's through the Wrigley Foundation and was soon signed by Middlesex. A tour of the West Indies with England Young Cricketers in 1976 and the award of a Middlesex county cap in 1978 seemed to indicate a bright future, but a subsequent poor season and Middlesex's signing of Paul Downton from Kent meant that he had to look elsewhere.

When Arnold Long retired at the end of the 1980 season, there was a vacancy in the wicket-keeping department at Sussex and Ian was keen to stay in the south of England. His first five years with the County were of sound achievement with the bat and behind the stumps and included, in 1985, his first hundred for the County, 101 against Leicestershire in a thrilling win by two wickets at the end of the season. In the following year John Barclay, the county captain, was plagued by injury and Ian, having been appointed vice-captain in 1985, found himself *de facto* captain for most of the season, which culminated in the winning of the NatWest Trophy against Lancashire at Lord's in September. The following season saw him promoted to county captain, but, sadly, he did not prosper in this role. Sussex finished last in the Championship, lost in the first round of the NatWest Trophy and ended near the bottom in the Sunday League. Although Ian took out his frustration on Northamptonshire with an amazing 111, including 5 sixes and 10 fours, at Hove in September, he resigned at the end of the season. He did, however, continue to play for the County for another three years before returning to Middlesex as Second XI captain for the 1991 season.

Ian gave sterling service to Sussex in limited overs matches, often opening the batting and scoring briskly. Had he possessed a touch more ability, he might have had a successful international career. He toured with England in Australia in 1982/83, but was unable, unsurprisingly, to edge out Bob Taylor from behind the stumps in the Tests. However, he did excel in the 1982/83 World Series in Australasia and in the 1983 World Cup in England, making a total of 18 appearances for his country, occasionally opening the batting and, from behind the stumps, dismissing 18 batsmen.

# Peter J. Graves
*LHB & SLA, 1965-80*

**Born:** Hove, 19 May 1946

**County Cap:** 1969

**Batting Record:**

| M | I | NO | Runs | Avge |
|---|---|---|---|---|
| 270 | 463 | 48 | 10,734 | 25.86 |
| *205* | *191* | *34* | *4,036* | *25.71* |
| **100** | **50** | | **CT/ST** | |
| 10 | 57 | | 198 | |
| *2* | *17* | | *60* | |

**Bowling Record:**

| O | M | Runs | W | Avge |
|---|---|---|---|---|
| 128 | 39 | 415 | 6 | 69.16 |
| **5wI** | **10wM** | | | |
| - | - | | | |

**Career Best Performances:**
145* v. Gloucestershire, Gloucester, 1974
*114* v. Cambridge University, Hove, 1974
(B&H)*
25-6-75-3 v. Gloucestershire, Cheltenham, 1965

Peter Graves was a pupil at Hove Manor School and, as soon as left, he joined Sussex groundstaff. He was soon playing for the Club and Ground sides and learning his craft under the watchful gaze of coaches James Langridge and George Cox. In 1965, he came into the County side and his first years were of relatively modest achievement, especially as he missed much of the 1967 season with glandular fever. The following season saw a further setback – against Middlesex at Lord's, the knuckle of his left index finger was broken and the resulting operation ended in complications. Unable to space his fingers correctly, he found himself unable to bowl and from then on had to concentrate solely on batting. Normally in the middle order, he was promoted to number four against the New Zealanders at Hove in 1969 and scored his first hundred for Sussex. 1970 saw him reach 1,000 runs for the first time, although this was only with the help of 2 fifties for the England Under-25 side at the Scarborough Festival.

From then on, his career started to make good progress. In 1971, he reached 1,000 runs for Sussex and in 1973 he had an average for limited-over matches – a form of the game at which he had not previously excelled – of over 47. By 1974 he was established as the County's regular number four in the order, heading the batting averages, making his highest scores in both forms of the game and being a quite exceptionally brilliant gully fielder.

Peter widened his experience by playing and coaching for the Orange Free State from 1969; in 1976, he scored 119 and 136 not out against Border in Bloemfontein. In 1975, he was appointed Sussex vice-captain, a post which he held until 1978. This was no sinecure, as Tony Greig was often absent on Test duty or engaged in negotiations for the Packer Circus, but his form was such that in 1978 he did not receive the captaincy, which went instead to Arnold Long. In any case it was his benefit year, and he immediately suffered another serious finger injury which kept him out of all but two Championship matches. By the end of the 1980 season constant injury to his hands led to his decision to retire. Peter's career might well have achieved much more; his considerable ability was not matched by the good fortune of many another cricketer.

# Anthony W. (Tony) Greig

*RHB & RM/OB, 1966-78*

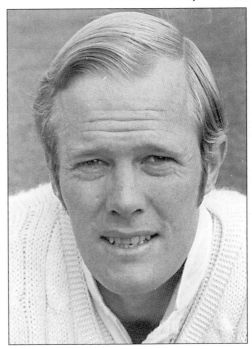

**Born:** Queenstown, South Africa, 6 October 1946

**County Cap:** 1967
**County Captain:** 1973-1977

**Batting Record:**

| M | I | NO | Runs | Avge |
|---|---|---|---|---|
| 209 | 358 | 21 | 9,528 | 28.27 |
| *154* | *144* | *13* | *3,299* | *25.18* |

| 100 | 50 | | CT/ST | |
|---|---|---|---|---|
| 14 | 51 | | 188 | |
| *3* | *19* | | *75* | |

**Bowling Record:**

| O | M | Runs | W | Avge |
|---|---|---|---|---|
| 5,081 | 1,186 | 14,541 | 509 | 28.56 |
| *1,150.1* | *115* | *4,638* | *209* | *22.19* |

| 5wI | 10wM | | | |
|---|---|---|---|---|
| 18 | 3 | | | |
| *2* | *-* | | | |

**Career Best Performances:**
226 v. Warwickshire, Hastings, 1975
*129 v. Yorkshire, Scarborough, 1976 (SL)*
19.1-8-25-8 v. Gloucestershire, Hove, 1967
*8-0-28-6 v. Middlesex, Hove, 1971 (SL)*

Tony Greig was one of the most influential figures in English cricket during the 1970s; sadly, he saw his reputation largely destroyed by his involvement in the 'Packer Affair', in which he, together with Greg Chappell, the former Australian Test captain, was seen as a recruiting officer for Kerry Packer's cricket circus.

From the day in May 1967 when Tony, in his first match for the County, returned to the Hove pavilion having scored 156 against a Lancashire attack including Brian Statham, Ken Higgs and Peter Lever, who were all England opening bowlers in their day, it was clear that a prodigy had arrived. Almost 6ft 8in tall and with fair good looks and an engaging manner, he exuded a charisma which immediately dominated any scene. The son of a Scottish father, an RAF officer who had been sent to South Africa in the Second World War to train pilots, and a South African mother, he had been educated at Queen's College, Queenstown. He had been recommended to Sussex by Richard Langridge, who was teaching there. His debut went on apace: his 156 in May was followed by 8 Gloucestershire wickets for 25 runs in July. At the end of his first season, still not past his twenty-first birthday, he had scored over 1,000 Championship runs and taken 63 wickets. His powerful upstanding batting and his medium-fast bowling delivered from his great height, which gained considerable lift from helpful pitches, started to attract attention outside the county circuit.

The seasons following his debut had produced similarly fine all-round figures and he was called in to play for England in the 1970 'Test' matches against the Rest of the World after the South African tour had been cancelled. It was strange, but he was not picked to play against India in 1971 and had to wait until the 1972 season to start his real Test career. He played in all five matches against Australia and topped England's batting averages. He bowled well too, and from that time onwards he became a fixture in England's Test team. In fact, he played 58 consecutive Test matches between 1972 and 1977 and captained England in 14 of these matches. His first three Test innings all went past the 50 mark; by the end of his career he had

*Tony Greig leads out the Sussex team v. West Indians at Hove in 1976.*

notched 8 Test hundreds (including a marvellous 110 against the might of Lillee and Thomson on an uneven pitch at Brisbane in 1974), had scored 3,599 runs and taken 141 wickets, including 13 in one match against West Indies in Trinidad in 1974, the highest number ever taken by an England player against the cricketers from the Caribbean.

Appointed County Captain in 1973, Tony continued to pull his weight for Sussex in Championship and limited-overs matches, enjoying considerable success in 1975, when he scored nearly 1,700 runs in all matches and 5 hundreds for Sussex, including a massive 226, with 6 sixes and 18 fours, against Warwickshire at Hastings. It was a fact, however, that Tony's efforts were often directed more towards England than towards his county. His leadership of England and his Test performances were bold, brave and belligerent, and of the 14 Tests in which he was in charge, often against Australia and the West Indies, three were won and only four lost. While his batting average for England was over 40, he could manage no better than 28 for his county and his captaincy of Sussex, while promising much, achieved very little. The County finished low down the table in all the years in which he was in charge and 1977 was

the best season – and his last – when they reached 8th position, but he played in only 12 matches.

By the mid-1970s, he had reached a peak of prosperity, both financially and in public esteem. He lived in a lavish house in Brighton, he drove a Jaguar provided by the Club's sponsors and he was England's and Sussex's captain. But this multi-talented and charming man also possessed a ruthless streak and was somewhat disingenuous. This latter characteristic led him to become involved with Kerry Packer's cricket circus. Charges of betrayal of trust resulted in his dismissal as England captain, his replacement as Sussex captain and his release from his county contract midway through 1978; he was still only thirty-two and could have given so much more on the cricket field. His potential to achieve was boundless, but the great idol was perceived to have feet of clay and was an embarrassment to all.

After he left Sussex, it became known that Tony was an epileptic and the fact that he mastered this disability in such a successful cricketing career softened the blow of the damage that he appeared to have done to the game of cricket.

# Ian A. Greig
*RHB & RM, 1980-85*

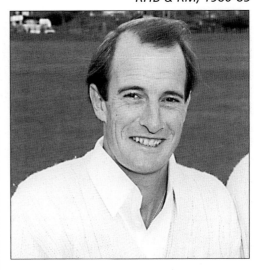

**Born:** Queenstown, South Africa, 8 December 1955

**County Cap:** 1981

**Batting Record:**

| M | I | NO | Runs | Avge |
|---|---|----|------|------|
| 107 | 137 | 20 | 3,155 | 26.96 |
| *105* | *90* | *16* | *1,519* | *20.53* |

| 100 | 50 | | CT/ST |
|-----|----|--|-------|
| 4 | 12 | | 76 |
| - | *2* | | *19* |

**Bowling Record:**

| O | M | Runs | W | Avge |
|---|---|------|---|------|
| 2,284 | 619 | 7,090 | 254 | 27.91 |
| *700.4* | *42* | *3,103* | *102* | *30.42* |

| 5wI | 10wM |
|-----|------|
| 7 | 2 |
| *2* | *-* |

**Career Best Performances:**
147* v. Oxford University, Oxford, 1983
*82 v. Warwickshire, Edgbaston, 1981 (NWT)*
22.4-6-43-7 v. Cambridge University, Cambridge, 1981
*11-1-35-5 v. Hampshire, Hove, 1981 (B&H)*

It was inevitable that Ian Greig would fall under the shadow of his elder brother, but he was a formidable all-round cricketer and, although less flamboyant than Tony, a strong and forceful character. Educated at Queen's College, Queenstown, Ian came in 1977 to Cambridge to read law, and immediately began to make his mark in University cricket. He gained blues in his first two years and became captain in 1979 when Oxford were defeated by an innings. *Wisden* commented: 'He was one of the most able of Cambridge captains of recent times.' At the same time, he managed to win two rugby blues.

Equally inevitably, perhaps, Ian joined Sussex and first played for them in 1980. He soon showed outstanding all-round skills: his medium-fast bowling, which had a good action and plenty of nip off the pitch, brought 76 wickets at 19 runs each in 1981. He also scored well over 900 runs. It was not unreasonable, therefore – although some commen-

tators expressed doubt – that he was selected for England in two Tests against Pakistan in 1982. Asked to open England's bowling, he returned exactly the same figures (4 for 53) as Tony had done in his first Test, but, although he bowled competently, his batting against spin was all at sea and his second Test proved to be his last. In 1983, Sussex engaged Dermot Reeve, his mirror image as a player, so there was immediate competition in the medium-fast department and in the middle-order batting. Although he had a good season in 1984, he was released 'on the grounds of economy' at the end of 1985. Reeve had apparently just edged ahead, but two years later the latter turned his back on Sussex and headed off to Warwickshire. Members were saddened that Ian had been let go two years earlier.

Consolation was, however, on hand. A call came from Brisbane where Ian was spending 1986/87 running a cricket school. Would he return to captain Surrey for the 1987 season? Of course, he leapt at the chance and proved himself a competent captain between 1987 and 1991, leading Surrey to success in Championship and one-day cricket. In 1990, he scored over 1,000 runs, including a huge 291 against Lancashire at The Oval. A knee injury hampered his bowling and after the 1991 season he gave up the captaincy, played a few games in 1992 and then joined his brother in Australia. Did the Sussex Committee make the right decision in 1985? One thinks perhaps not.

# Stewart C. (Billy) Griffith *CBE DFC TD*
*RHB & WK, 1937-54*

**Born:** Wandsworth, London, 6 June 1914
**Died:** Felpham, 7 April 1993

**County Captain:** 1946

**Batting Record:**

| M | I | NO | Runs | Avge |
|---|---|----|------|------|
| 122 | 194 | 16 | 2,991 | 16.80 |
| **100** | **50** | | **CT/ST** | |
| 2 | 10 | | 187/39 | |

**Bowling Record:**

| O | M | Runs | W | Avge |
|---|---|------|---|------|
| 3 | 0 | 23 | 0 | -- |
| **5wI** | **10wM** | | | |
| - | - | | | |

**Career Best Performances:**
111 v. Nottinghamshire, Hastings, 1949
Best season: 1947 (48 dismissals, ct 42 and st 6)

Stewart Griffith, always known as 'Billy', served the game of cricket over a lifetime in a variety of capacities that are hard to match. He was successively, or in some cases concurrently, university, county and Test cricketer, schoolmaster, secretary, captain and president of Sussex, *Sunday Times* cricket correspondent; and assistant secretary, secretary and president of MCC.

Educated at Dulwich College and Cambridge University, he won a wicket-keeping blue in 1935, was a member of the MCC side which toured Australasia in 1935/36, and he first played for Sussex in 1937. After teaching at Dulwich, he found himself at war in the Glider Pilot Regiment, serving in Normandy and at Arnhem and reaching the rank of Lieutenant-Colonel. In 1945, he kept wicket for England in the five 'Victory' Test matches against the Australian Services and he looked set for a long England career.

In 1946, he became captain-secretary of Sussex but, despite his sterling efforts, Sussex ended bottom of the Championship. He decided, therefore, to retain the secretary's post but to hand over the captaincy to Hugh Bartlett for 1947. His form with the gloves was such that he was selected for the 1947/48

MCC side to the West Indies. Pressed into service as an opening batsman in the Second Test in Trinidad, he batted throughout the day for 110 not out and went on to score 140. It was the first case of a batsman scoring his maiden first-class hundred in a Test match, but it did him little good. Poor form elsewhere in the party led to Len Hutton joining the tour soon afterwards. In the following winter, as vice-captain in the MCC side in South Africa, he displaced Godfrey Evans as England's wicketkeeper in the last two Tests. After that, his active cricketing career was with Sussex, for whom he last played in 1954.

In 1952, Billy was appointed assistant secretary of MCC and he became secretary ten years later. From then onwards, Lord's was the centre of his life. His stewardship of the post, amid the enormous changes in cricket in the 1960s, was characterised by his amiable and common sense nature, even in trying circumstances. He retired as secretary in 1974 and became president in 1979. Asked by the ICC to revise the laws of the game, he produced the 1980 code. Yet he had not forgotten Sussex; at the request of Lavinia, Duchess of Norfolk, he ensured the continuance of cricket at Arundel, surely one of the County's most idyllic settings.

**Born:** Beaconsfield, Buckinghamshire, 25 November 1943

**County Cap:** 1967
**County Captain** 1968-1972

**Batting Record:**

| M | I | NO | Runs | Avge |
|---|---|----|------|------|
| 232 | 386 | 85 | 7,533 | 25.02 |
| *119* | *107* | *27* | *1,675* | *20.94* |

| 100 | 50 | CT/ST |
|-----|-----|-------|
| 5 | 37 | 196/6 |
| - | *1* | *56/1* |

**Bowling Record:**

| O | M | Runs | W | Avge |
|---|---|------|---|------|
| 10 | 3 | 24 | 0 | -- |

| 5wM | 10wM |
|-----|------|
| - | - |

**Career Best Performances:**
158 v. Cambridge University, Hove, 1969
*61 v. Northants, Kettering, 1970 (SL)*

Mike Griffith probably did not find it easy to follow in his father's footsteps. One rarely does. At Marlborough, he scored five centuries in his career and over 1,000 runs (average 97.00) in 1961 before moving on to Cambridge to win a blue at cricket in each of his three years and blues for both hockey and rackets.

After a few games in 1962, Mike played in Sussex's 1964 Gillette cup-winning team and kept wicket and scored 50 in each innings against the Australians, causing Wally Grout, the Aussie 'keeper, to rate him as the best young gloveman in England. Sadly, his 'keeping was restricted by the presence of Jim Parks, almost a fixture behind the stumps in England's side in the 1960s. Yet he batted well for the County and four years after his first encounter he scored a hundred against the Australians.

In 1968, Sussex was experiencing one of its unhappy periods and Jim Parks, appointed captain in 1967, resigned the post half-way through the season, saying that he was at odds with his team-mates. Mike had a lot on his plate at the time; in the winter of 1967/68 he had represented England at hockey against Belgium and was in the Olympic squad. He now found the Sussex captaincy being offered to him at the age of twenty-four, something he was not expecting nor adequately prepared for. Having consulted his father and confirmed that the Sussex Committee's offer was unanimous, he decided to accept. It proved a hard task. Sussex finished bottom of the Championship in 1968, although they did reach the final of the Gillette Cup.

Under his leadership, the County did somewhat better over the next three years. He personally had an excellent year in 1971 when he headed Sussex's Championship averages and scored 142 not out against Nottinghamshire. It remained, however, an unhappy time. There was talk of a drift towards anarchy in the dressing room and, on one occasion when Mike had to pursue a recalcitrant bowler marching silently towards the boundary, it looked rather like insubordination. He was not the sort of character who relished confrontation and in 1972, after the County had finished next to bottom in the Championship, he resigned the captaincy and handed over to Tony Greig. There was, however, very much more good to be said about Mike Griffith than about some of his team.

# Herbert E. (Jim) Hammond
*RHB & RFM, 1928-46*

**Born:** Brighton, 7 November 1907
**Died:** Brighton, 16 June 1985

**Batting Record:**

| M | I | NO | Runs | Avge |
|---|---|----|------|------|
| 196 | 267 | 40 | 4,251 | 18.72 |
| **100** | **50** | | **CT/ST** | |
| 1 | 19 | | 170 | |

**Bowling Record:**

| O | M | Runs | W | Avge |
|---|---|------|---|------|
| 4,421 | 789 | 12,290 | 428 | 28.71 |
| **5wI** | **10wM** | | | |
| 16 | 1 | | | |

**Career Best Performances:**
103* v. Warwickshire, Edgbaston, 1936
33-13-76-8 v. Surrey, Oval, 1934

Most counties have in their ranks a hard-working, reliable, but, in terms of cricketing statistics, relatively undistinguished cricketer, a player not in the top flight, but one who always gives of his all. One such cricketer was Jim Hammond for Sussex.

Born in the Seven Dials district of Brighton, he was a reserve for England boys and, at the age of sixteen, started playing club cricket in Brighton and Hove. At the same time he was playing soccer for Lewes and in that period he gained one England international cap when he played against Wales at Cardiff. In 1928, when he was twenty-two, he decided to become a professional sportsman, joining Sussex and signing up with Fulham FC, who apparently offered better terms than Brighton and Hove Albion.

His first few years with Sussex were relatively barren – he missed the whole of the 1929 season owing to an operation for appendicitis – and, although he played 20 matches for the County in 1930 and was noted by no lesser judges than Ranji and A.C. MacLaren as a cricketer of some promise, it was not until 1934 that he gained a regular place in the County side. From that time onwards he often opened the bowling and, on some occasions, the batting as well. In 1934 he took 8 wickets in an innings on a fast pitch against Surrey at the Oval and in 1936 he scored the only century of his career when, batting with Jim Parks senior, who made 104, he took part in an unfinished opening partnership of 214 against Warwickshire at Edgbaston, his own score being 103. Jim continued to be part and parcel of Sussex's team up until the Second World War, taking his best haul of wickets – 85 Championship and 91 overall – in 1937 when he was the County's leading bowler.

When the Second World War arrived in 1939, Jim joined the RAF and rose to the rank of Flight Lieutenant. On demobilisation, he came back to Sussex for one final season and after that began a coaching career which took him to Holland and then to Cheltenham College from 1947 to 1960. In the following season he joined the list of first-class umpires and remained in this post until the 1964 season, when he accepted a post as coach at Brighton College. This lasted until 1974, when he handed over to another Sussex cricketer, Ian Thomson.

# Arthur B. and Jesse B. Hide

*LHB & LM, 1882-90 and RHB & RF, 1876-93*

**Arthur B. Hide**
**Born:** Eastbourne, 7 May 1860
**Died:** Bexhill, 5 November 1933
**Batting Record:**

| M | I | NO | Runs | Avge |
|---|---|----|------|------|
| 113 | 192 | 39 | 1,107 | 7.24 |

| 100 | 50 | | CT/ST | |
|-----|----|--|-------|--|
| - | - | | 72 | |

**Bowling Record:**

| O | M | Runs | W | Avge |
|---|---|------|---|------|
| 5,640 | 2,760 | 7,598 | 398 | 19.09 |

| 5wI | 10wM | | | |
|-----|------|--|--|--|
| 20 | 1 | | | |

**Career Best Performances:**
45 v. Kent, Tonbridge, 1886
38.2-16-44-7 v. Surrey, Hove, 1888
(4 balls to the over)

**Jesse B. Hide**
**Born:** Eastbourne, 12 March 1857
**Died:** Edinburgh, 19 March 1924
**Batting Record:**

| M | I | NO | Runs | Avge |
|---|---|----|------|------|
| 155 | 286 | 19 | 4,408 | 16.50 |

| 100 | 50 | | CT/ST | |
|-----|----|--|-------|--|
| 4 | 13 | | 101 | |

**Bowling Record:**

| O | M | Runs | W | Avge |
|---|---|------|---|------|
| 5,005 | 2,616 | 8,780 | 406 | 21.63 |

| 5wI | 10wM | | | |
|-----|------|--|--|--|
| 19 | 4 | | | |

**Career Best Performances:**
173 v. Kent, Hove, 1886
33-14-47-8 v. Lancashire, Old Trafford, 1885
(4 balls to the over)

The Hide brothers hailed from Eastbourne and when they were not playing cricket they reverted to the family calling of fishing in Pevensey Bay. Jesse (on the right in the picture) was the elder and he first played for Sussex in 1876. He was a hard-hitting middle-order batsman and a fast right-hand round-arm bowler whose best cricket came after he returned to England from his post with the South Australia Cricket Association between 1879 and 1882. In Adelaide his influence as a coach became immediately evident and his daily sessions were regularly attended by the club players. When he returned to Sussex he had some good seasons in the 1880s, making hundreds against Kent, Cambridge University and Gloucestershire between 1884 and 1888 and taking over 50 wickets in 1886. Two bowling feats stand out: playing for Fifteen of South Australia in 1882 against the Australian XI of that year, he bowled 64 balls for one run – quite an achievement against a strong team – and in 1890 for Sussex versus MCC at Lord's he took 4 wickets in 4 balls. He played for Cornwall after he left Sussex and ended his days in Edinburgh.

Arthur, younger by three years, was a less well-known cricketer than his brother and while certainly a less able batsman, he was probably the better bowler. He came into the Sussex side at the age of twenty-two in 1882 and retained his place in the side for nine seasons, before moving on to Marlborough College as a coach. His medium-pace left-arm bowling earned him slightly fewer wickets than his brother, but at a more favourable average. He was often close to 50 wickets a season and in 1888 – his best season – he took 81 wickets and often produced match analyses which look nowadays, notwithstanding the fact that there were in his time mainly 4-ball overs, extraordinarily frugal. In 1886, in the match against the Australians, he bowled 98 overs with 50 maidens and took 4 wickets for 105 runs.

# Albert J. (Jack) Holmes *AFC and Bar*
*RHB & RM, 1922-39*

**Born:** Thornton Heath, Surrey, 30 June 1899
**Died:** Burwash, 21 May 1950

**County Captain:** 1936-1939

**Batting Record:**

| M | I | NO | Runs | Avge |
|---|---|---|---|---|
| 203 | 311 | 23 | 6,110 | 21.21 |
| **100** | **50** | | **CT/ST** | |
| 6 | 23 | | 118 | |

**Bowling Record:**

| O | M | Runs | W | Avge |
|---|---|---|---|---|
| 110 | 20 | 354 | 8 | 44.25 |
| **5wI** | **10wM** | | | |
| - | - | | | |

**Career Best Performances:**
133* v Nottinghamshire, Hove, 1938
1-0-2-1 v. Worcestershire, Eastbourne, 1939

Jack Holmes gained a distinguished sporting reputation at Repton School, served with the RFC in the First World War and then went into business. In 1923, his second season with Sussex, he scored over 1,000 runs, but he then played on relatively few occasions until 1936. The reason for this gap was that he had rejoined the RAF in 1925 and, having made a name for himself as an instructor, he retired in 1935 with the rank of Flight Lieutenant, a title he retained as a form of address. When Alan Melville returned to South Africa, Jack was an obvious candidate for the Sussex captaincy in 1936 and he led the County until 1939 – he was 'one of the finest captains Sussex ever had', to quote Sir Home Gordon, a great Sussex supporter and president in 1948.

Jack was a powerful and aggressive batsman who made most of his runs in front of the wicket. He loved an uphill fight, but he could also offer watchful defence. When he reached 1,000 runs in 1937, he had achieved the feat fourteen seasons after the first occasion, which in itself must be unique. In that year of success, he was associated with Tommy Cook in an unbroken fifth-wicket stand of 226 against Leicestershire, when his own contribution was 122.

An able leader, he managed the MCC side to South Africa in 1938/39, and *Wisden* in its report noted how successful the tour had been and added 'with none more judicious in all his responsibilities than Flight Lieutenant A.J. Holmes, the manager.' He was then invited to captain the MCC tour to India in the winter of 1939/40, which was cancelled owing to the Second World War.

Recalled to the RAF as a Wing Commander, Jack became the RAF's Chief Flying Instructor and ended the war in the rank of Group Captain. He later served on many committees and was chairman of Sussex CCC. In 1939, he had become a Test selector and was chairman from 1946 until 1949, when ill health caused his resignation and led to his early death, at the age of fifty. Not long before his death the Sussex Committee asked him to give Hugh Bartlett the news of his replacement as captain, but when he returned to Brighton to report to Billy Griffith, the secretary, he replied: 'We chatted over old times, but I am sorry, I just hadn't the heart to tell him.' Such a man was Jack Holmes.

# Walter A. Humphreys

*RHB & RH lobs, 1871-96*

**Born:** Southsea, Hampshire, 28 October 1849
**Died:** Brighton, 23 March 1924

**Batting Record:**

| M | I | NO | Runs | Avge |
|---|---|---|------|------|
| 248 | 440 | 80 | 5,806 | 16.12 |

| 100 | 50 | | CT/ST | |
|-----|----|--|-------|--|
| 1 | 16 | | 191 | |

**Bowling Record:**

| Runs | W | Avge |
|------|---|------|
| 14,137 | 682 | 20.72 |

| 5wI | 10wM |
|-----|------|
| 49 | 8 |

**Career Best Performances:**
117 v. Cambridge University, Hove, 1887
28.2-3-83-8 v. Middlesex, Hove, 1893

Hampshire-born Walter Humphreys came to Sussex at a young age and has always been regarded as a Sussex cricketer. His importance to Sussex cricket stems from his skill as an under-arm lob bowler, and he was probably the finest exponent of this style of bowling in the world at the end of the nineteenth century.

Known as 'Cobbler' Humphreys, he made shoes and boots at 67, Upper North Street, Brighton. In 1871, the County selectors heard of his performances in Brighton club cricket, in which he once scored 176 not out on the College ground. He mostly played for Brighton Brunswick and in the late 1870s he twice took all ten wickets in an innings, while in 1885, playing for Sheffield Park in a club match against Birch Grove, he scored 239. He was also a keen footballer and once scored 31 goals in a season for the Brighton Rangers club.

In his early days with the County, however, he did not bowl, but batted steadily, fielded well and occasionally kept wicket. A full nine years passed, therefore, before he experimented with his under-arm lobs in first-class cricket. In 1880 he took 5 wickets for 74 against Surrey and did the hat-trick against the Australians. After three relatively barren years, he came back in 1884 to torment the Australians again with a further hat-trick and,

another four years later, he was instrumental in defeating the tourists by 58 runs, his own share being 5 for 21 and 4 for 19. The culmination of his career probably occurred in 1893, when he took 148 wickets for Sussex in all matches at just over 17 each, but the Test selectors ignored him until the 1894/95 tour of Australia. He was then past his best and only played in the up-country fixtures and never in a Test match. For Sussex, however, he had continued to do well in the early 1890s, taking 8 wickets in an innings on five occasions, often with a field setting that placed almost all the fielders on the on-side. Billy Murdoch, who made 286 not out against Sussex in 1882, paid him a high compliment by saying: 'Even when I had made 200, I couldn't tell from watching his hand which way he meant to turn the ball.'

Leaving Sussex in 1896, he played the odd game for Hampshire, the county of his birth, before retiring and living in Brighton for the remainder of his life.

# Imran Khan Niazi
*RHB & RF, 1977-88*

**Born:** Lahore, Pakistan, 25 November 1952

**County Cap:** 1978

**Batting Record:**

| M | I | NO | Runs | Avge |
|---|---|---|---|---|
| 131 | 212 | 42 | 7,329 | 43.11 |
| *164* | *158* | *24* | *4,298* | *32.07* |
| **100** | **50** | | **CT/ST** | |
| 13 | 44 | | 32 | |
| *3* | *28* | | *33* | |

**Bowling Record:**

| O | M | Runs | W | Avge |
|---|---|---|---|---|
| 3,224 | 808 | 8,169 | 409 | 19.97 |
| *1241.2* | *173* | *4,059* | *209* | *19.42* |
| **5wI** | **10wM** | | | |
| 20 | 1 | | | |
| *2* | - | | | |

**Career Best Performances:**
167 v. Gloucestershire, Hove, 1978
*114* v. Nottinghamshire, Hove, 1983 (NWT)*
14.3-4-34-8 v. Middlesex, Lord's, 1986
*7.3-2-8-5 v. Northamptonshire, Northampton, 1978 (B&H)*

Imran Khan was an influential cricketer at most stages of his eminent career. Educated at Aitcheson College, Lahore, and Worcester Royal Grammar School, he began his English career with Worcestershire in 1971. He won three blues at Oxford, captaining them in 1974 and being the most outstanding university cricketer of his generation. Although capped by Worcestershire in 1976, he seemed unhappy at New Road and was pleased to come to Hove in 1977. He had begun his Test career as early as 1971, when he was only eighteen, but, although a regular Test player, it was not until 1982 that he began his long reign as Pakistan captain. He became not only a captain who could hold together the disparate factions in Pakistan's cricket, but the greatest of their all-rounders and a figure of immense importance and influence, almost a household name, in world cricket.

Sussex were certainly fortunate to acquire his services. Although there were times when injury and the exigencies of his country's Test team meant that he was unavailable for the County, he always made his presence felt whenever he was able to turn out. It was perhaps because of his other commitments that he was not invited to captain the County. For if he had done so,

there can be little doubt that he would have been a great success. By his standards at least, his Sussex career made a slow start in 1977, but in the following year he made the most runs and took the most wickets in Championship matches and scored an impressive 167 against Gloucestershire, with 104 of his runs coming in boundaries. When the South African, Garth le Roux, began to play regularly for the County in 1980, he and Imran combined into a most potent opening attack. In 1981, when Sussex failed by a whisker to lift what would have been their first Championship pennant, the pairing of Imran and le Roux, backed up by Ian Greig and Geoff Arnold, took 147 wickets between them and was a significant factor in the County's success. In three of his seasons with Sussex, he led both the Championship batting and bowling averages. Constant cricket – Imran had been a prominent member of the Kerry Packer circus in the late 1970s – was beginning to take its toll on his shins. In 1983, barely fit as the result of his injuries, he was called upon to bowl fourth

Left: *Imran showing his batting prowess in 1985.* Right: *As Pakistani captain, Imran bowling against Sussex in 1987.*

change for the County in an end-of-season encounter with Warwickshire at Edgbaston. In 4 overs and 3 balls he took 6 wickets for 6 runs, including a hat-trick, and the home county went from 156 for 4 to 218 all out. Sadly, even Imran's well made 54 in Sussex's second innings could not prevent the County losing by 21 runs.

His contribution to Sussex's limited-overs cricket was no less important. He played his part in the 1978 Gillette Cup success and eight years later, when the County won the NatWest Trophy, his 50 not out, achieved with what *Wisden* described as 'casual elegance', saw his side comfortably home with fewer than two overs to spare.

Imran's time in cricket coincided in part with the careers of three other great all-rounders, Ian Botham of England, Kapil Dev of India and New Zealand's Sir Richard Hadlee. Pundits have doubtless passed fruitful evenings extolling the virtues of their particular hero, and who can be sure which argument is the strongest? The case for Imran, however, can be compelling. His bowling, with its magnificent high leap, was genuinely fast and his batting was technically sounder than that of any of the others. He was often outspoken in defence of fast bowlers' use of the bouncer and was happy to employ it himself, but as a batsman he was also prepared to swallow his own medicine and produced match-winning performances in both his roles.

By 1988, Imran was approaching his thirty-sixth birthday. He managed only four Championship matches for Sussex, but honoured his promise to help with limited-overs matches. The time for less cricket had arrived. Although he continued in Test cricket until 1991 and led Pakistan to victory over England in the final of the Benson & Hedges World Cup in 1992, with his own 72 being the highest score on either side, his disenchantment with domestic cricket at home or abroad was complete and he moved quietly away from the game.

After the death of his mother from cancer in 1985, he began a massive fund-raising campaign to build a specialist hospital in Lahore and the image he created helped him to move into Pakistani politics, although he has yet to make a significant mark. Well-liked by women, he eschewed an arranged Pakistani marriage and in 1995, perhaps to the surprise of some, married Jemima, the daughter of the late financier, James Goldsmith.

# Albert E. (Ted) James
*RHB & RM, 1948-60*

**Born:** Newport Longville, Buckinghamshire, 7 August 1924

**County Cap:** 1950

**Batting Record:**

| M | I | NO | Runs | Avge |
|---|---|----|------|------|
| 299 | 414 | 135 | 3,411 | 12.22 |
| **100** | **50** | | **CT/ST** | |
| - | 4 | | 111 | |

**Bowling Record:**

| O | M | Runs | W | Avge |
|---|---|------|---|------|
| 9,994 | 3,295 | 22,841 | 843 | 27.09 |

**Career Best Performances:**
63* v. Nottinghamshire, Trent Bridge, 1950
33.5-13-60-9 v. Yorkshire, Hove, 1955

Ted James learned his cricket initially on a Buckinghamshire village green, progressing later into his county's side in the Minor Counties' Championship. While appearing in a pre-season trial he was spotted by A.D.G. Matthews, the former Glamorgan and Northamptonshire player, who was then the cricket master at Stowe School. Matthews had always kept his ear to the ground and knew that the Sussex attack was certainly not the strongest in the country. Ted was, therefore, given a trial by Sussex and registered for the 1948 season.

In his first match against Yorkshire at Bramall Lane, Sheffield, Sussex had collapsed to 78 in the first innings and the hosts amassed 309 for 5 wickets before declaring with Len Hutton 176 not out. Ted had bowled his off-breaks accurately and in the course of 35 overs had taken 4 for 97, including bowling Norman Yardley first ball – an England captain whose career was not yet over. When the side returned to the pavilion, he inquired to the raucous amusement of his team-mates: 'Who was that fellow who got

the 176?' At the end of the season, he had taken 33 wickets at 25 each and was top of the averages. In the following season he was perhaps less successful, but a turning point in his career came in 1950, when Jim Wood was not available and Sussex lacked a seam bowler. Rather in the way that Maurice Tate had converted with astonishing results from off-spin to medium-pace seam, Ted did the same. His leg-cutters were so effective that in the following ten seasons he formed the backbone of the County's attack and took over 750 wickets, his 111 in 1955 being his best return. During his career, apart from his first two years and his last, he never failed to take 50 wickets in a season and, on many occasions, considerably more. He had some startling analyses to his credit: in 1951, he bowled Hampshire out for 118, his own return being 19.3 overs, 12 maidens and 7 wickets for 12 runs. Four years later, when Sussex defeated Yorkshire at Hove, he took 9 wickets for 60 in the course of 33 overs.

He was no novice as a batsman and his sound defensive technique often helped the County out of a precarious position and, because of his stubborn method, he occasionally opened the Sussex innings. Never a real star, Ted typified the loyal and reliable county professional.

# Javed Miandad Khan
*RHB & LBG, 1976-79*

**Born:** Karachi, Pakistan, 12 June 1957

**County Cap:** 1977

**Batting Record:**

| M | I | NO | Runs | Avge |
|---|---|----|------|------|
| 40 | 67 | 11 | 2,511 | 44.83 |
| *49* | *49* | *10* | *1,300* | *33.33* |

| 100 | 50 | | CT/ST |
|-----|----|--|-------|
| 7 | 13 | | 47 |
| - | *9* | | *18* |

**Bowling Record:**

| O | M | Runs | W | Avge |
|---|---|------|---|------|
| 243 | 36 | 941 | 22 | 42.77 |
| *4* | *0* | *24* | *1* | *24.00* |

**Career Best Performances:**
162 v. Kent, Canterbury, 1976
*98* v. Lancashire, Hastings, 1979 (SL)*
5.2-2-10-4 v. Northamptonshire, Northampton, 1977
*2-0-12-1 v. Warwickshire, Hove, 1976 (GC)*

An uninformed spectator of the county scene might have found it surprising, even bizarre, that a county was prepared to discard a batsman who had scored 311 for Karachi Whites against National Bank at the age of seventeen, had become the youngest player to score a Test double-hundred when he was only nineteen and had registered six Test centuries before his twenty-second birthday. Yet this is what Sussex did with Javed Miandad in 1979. The reason, if viewed clearly and logically, gradually becomes obvious. There was a glut of overseas players at Hove and Garth le Roux and Kepler Wessels were considered better long-term bets.

Javed joined the Sussex staff in 1976 after a period of qualification in which he scored 227 for Sussex Second XI versus Hampshire and sent his opponents home gasping at his magical ability. He played in only five matches in 1976, but was able to come top of the Sussex averages and fourth in the national list. An innings of 162 versus Kent entertained the Canterbury crowd, while 7 sixes and 16 fours sped to the boundary in only three hours and twenty-five minutes. The 1977 season, in which he amassed more than 1,300 runs and averaged over 40, was really his only full and proper year with the County, and the next two seasons were stop-go affairs despite some excellent performances in the limited-overs game. It was not surprising, therefore, that he went to Glamorgan for the 1980 season. In his second season there he scored 2,083 runs (average 69.43) and notched a record eight hundreds. By the time he left the Welsh county in 1985, he had scored over 6,500 first-class runs and 17 centuries and passed 3,000 runs in limited-overs matches.

The rest is history. Three Test scores of over 250 – Bradman managed five, some others have reached two – over 3,000 runs and 8 hundreds more than any other Pakistani Test batsman. There must be even more to say, but Sussex apparently felt that Imran's all-round talent, allied to the fast bowling of le Roux, together with the pugnacious batting of Kepler Wessels, fitted the bill rather more adequately. It may also have happened that other players trained more regularly than Javed and generally fitted in better. But the thought is bound to linger on – what if?

57

# Vallance W.C. Jupp
*RHB & RMF/OB, 1909-22*

**Born:** Burgess Hill, 27 March 1891
**Died:** Spratton, Northamptonshire, 9 July 1960

**Batting Record:**

| M | I | NO | Runs | Avge |
|---|---|----|------|------|
| 173 | 294 | 39 | 7,452 | 29.22 |
| **100** | **50** | | **CT/ST** | |
| 14 | 33 | | 78 | |

**Bowling Record:**

| O | M | Runs | W | Avge |
|---|---|------|---|------|
| 2,458 | 477 | 7,868 | 351 | 22.41 |
| **5wI** | **10wM** | | | |
| 21 | 2 | | | |

**Career Best Performances:**
217* v. Worcestershire, Worcester, 1914
13-4-38-7 v. Hampshire, Hove, 1920

Sussex must always feel that they did not get their full return on Vallance Jupp. Educated at St John's School, Burgess Hill, he captained the First XI and in his last year averaged more than 100 with the bat. When a player dropped out suddenly he was summoned from Brighton to Leyton in 1909 to make his debut against Essex. He batted at number 10, made 28 not out in a crisis and added 68 for the last wicket with Harry Butt. He did not develop as rapidly as expected and in his first three seasons he batted down the order and did not bowl regularly, although he took a hat-trick against Surrey in 1911. In 1913, however, he started to find some real form and, moving up the order, made his maiden hundred, 112 against Northamptonshire. Even better things were to follow and in the next season he scored over 1,600 runs and reached 217 not out against Worcestershire, while heading the Championship bowling with 51 wickets. A talented and powerful all-rounder was in the making.

Vallance served in the Royal Engineers during the First World War before transfer-

ring to the RAF in 1918. When he returned to Sussex in 1919, it was as an amateur and, after a moderate first season, he began to show that an absence of four years had not impaired his skill. In 1920, he scored nearly 1,400 runs for Sussex and, having turned from a bowler of just above medium pace to an off-spinner, took 108 wickets, thus completing the first of his ten doubles – more than any other amateur has done and exceeded only by the Yorkshire professionals Hirst and Rhodes – although eight of these were achieved after he had moved to Northamptonshire. One season later he played two Tests for England against Australia. His brilliant batting fell a few runs short of 2,000 for the County; he totalled seven hundreds, including 179 against Leicestershire and he took 114 wickets. Much ability was clearly in store, but not, sadly, for Sussex.

He had business interests in Northampton and in 1922 he accepted the offer of the county's secretaryship. Although he had to qualify for his new county, he was still able to tour South Africa in 1922/23 and play four more Tests. He then began a highly successful career in the Midlands, played two more Tests for England and captained his new county between 1927 and 1931, not retiring until 1938.

# Ernest H. Killick
*LHB & RM/SRA, 1893-1913*

**Born:** Horsham, 17 January 1875
**Died:** Hove, 29 September 1948

**Batting Record:**

| M | 1 | NO | Runs | Avge |
|---|---|----|------|------|
| 450 | 752 | 52 | 18,539 | 26.48 |
| **100** | **50** | | **CT/ST** | |
| 22 | 92 | | 182 | |

**Bowling Record:**

| O | M | Runs | W | Avge |
|---|---|------|---|------|
| 7,101 | 1,770 | 19,765 | 723 | 27.33 |
| **5wI** | **10wM** | | | |
| 25 | 1 | | | |

**Career Best Performances:**
200 v. Yorkshire, Hove, 1901
7.2-2-10-7 v. Essex, Leyton, 1910

For over fifty years Ernest Killick was closely connected with Sussex County Cricket Club. Aged eighteen, he joined the County in 1893 and scored for them after his retirement for many years, even occasionally after the Second World War. Although a Horsham club wicketkeeper, he joined Sussex as a bowler. His first three years did not produce any significant results, but at Hove he met Alfred Shaw, the former Nottinghamshire bowler, who recognised his batting talent. In 1896, besides taking 47 wickets, he passed 1,000 runs for the season, having made only 102 runs in the previous three summers. Of particular merit was his innings against Somerset at Taunton when, going in at 4th wicket down, he was last out for 191, having hit 26 fours.

But it was not all beer and skittles. His sight started to give him trouble and in 1897 he lost his place in the side, but in the following year he reappeared with spectacles and made 77 against Surrey. From that date, 11 July 1898, he played in 391 consecutive matches for Sussex until his retirement in 1913. His success went on apace, and in 1901 he was involved in two famous partnerships at Hove: against Lancashire he scored 119 in a partnership of 298 with Ranji (204), which remains a Sussex record for the 3rd wicket; two matches later, against Yorkshire, he and

C.B. Fry (209) put on 349 for the 2nd wicket, Ernest's share being exactly 200. *Wisden* commented that, although he was lucky at the start of his innings, 'afterwards, cutting brilliantly, he played a distinctly brighter game than his famous partner'. He passed 1,000 runs in ten seasons, 1906 with 1,767 runs being his best return, and in 1905 he did the double by scoring 1,338 runs and taking 107 wickets.

His bowling suffered the extremes of fortune. He took 4 for 2 against Nottinghamshire in 1905, 5 for 2 against Hampshire in 1907 and 7 for 10 against Essex in 1910. At Tunbridge Wells in 1911, he bowled unchanged for four-and-three-quarter hours, delivering 56 overs with 23 maidens and taking 4 for 95. On the other hand, he was one of the victims of Ted Alletson at Hove in 1911, when he took 1 for 130, including one over (including two no-balls) which went for 34 – 46604446.

On retirement he became County scorer and enjoyed his hobbies, especially music, for which he had a real talent.

# R. James Kirtley
*RHB & RFM, 1995-*

**Born:** Eastbourne, 10 January 1975

**County Cap:** 1998

**Batting Record:**

| M | I | NO | Runs | Avge |
|---|---|---|---|---|
| 85 | 124 | 37 | 923 | 10.61 |
| *94* | *42* | *22* | *213* | *10.65* |
| 100 | 50 | | CT/ST | |
| - | 2 | | 25 | |
| - | - | | 25 | |

**Bowling Record:**

| O | M | R | W | Avge |
|---|---|---|---|---|
| 2,770 | 607 | 8,198 | 309 | 26.53 |
| *694.2* | *46* | *3192* | *141* | *22.64* |

| 5wI | 10wM |
|---|---|
| 16 | 3 |
| *1* | - |

**Career Best Performances:**
59 v. Durham, Eastbourne, 1998
*17* v. Somerset, Hove, 1999 (SL)*
14.1-6-21-7 v. Hampshire, Southampton, 1999
*12-2-39-5 v. Shropshire, Hove, 1997 (NWT)*

James Kirtley, who was educated at Clifton College but was a Sussex Young Cricketer, made his first-class debut in 1995. A year later, still on the fringe of the County side but selected for the TCCB XI playing South Africa 'A' at Chester-le-Street, he took 8 wickets in what was only his fifth first-class match. The following winter he joined Mashonaland in Zimbabwe and, when England were on their infamous visit there, he played in the side that defeated the tourists by 7 wickets, claiming 5 wickets for 53 in the first innings, including England captain, Michael Atherton – 'an unusual, but effective way of getting noticed by the Selectors,' as *Wisden*, somewhat tongue in cheek, commented.

By 1998, James was an integral part of the County side, forming a formidable opening attack with Jason Lewry. His 54 wickets included a remarkable 7 for 29 against Nottinghamshire in which Sussex scraped home, losing 6 wickets when requiring only 74 to win. Later, he showed that he could bat too, making 59 against Durham at Eastbourne. His progress was swift from then on: 65 wickets in 1999 saw him selected for the England 'A' tour of Bangladesh and New Zealand in the following winter. He played in all four 'Test' matches and claimed 19 first-class wickets (average 19.36). 1999 and 2000 were again successful seasons for him, but a cloud was appearing on the horizon. His faster ball was being questioned.

Examination by the ECB cleared him of any illegality and 2001 saw him promoted to Sussex vice-captain and leading the side with considerable success at the beginning of a season in which he ended up the leading wicket-taker in English first-class cricket with 75 at 23.32 each. Not only was he a fearsome opening bowler in the longer game, but he was earning a reputation in limited-overs cricket as a bowler who was not only able to swing the new ball, but could also bowl effectively 'at the death'. Unsurprisingly, he was selected for England's limited-overs side that toured Zimbabwe so effectively in October 2001. Sadly, in the course of the matches in which he was doing well, the match referee decided, without any report from the umpires, to investigate James' faster ball. Although he completed the tour, he was not selected for any further representative cricket in the winter of 2001/02 and while the chairman of selectors asserts that James' action has had no effect on selection, Sussex supporters tend to view things rather differently.

# James Langridge
*LHB & SLA, 1924-53*

**Born:** Chailey, 10 July 1906
**Died:** Withdean, Brighton, 10 September 1966

**County Cap:** 1927
**County Captain:** 1950-1952

**Batting Record:**

| M | I | NO | Runs | Avge |
|---|---|----|------|------|
| 622 | 955 | 142 | 28,894 | 35.55 |

| 100 | 50 | CT/ST |
|-----|-----|-------|
| 39 | 169 | 345 |

**Bowling Record:**

| O | M | Runs | W | Avge |
|---|---|------|---|------|
| 13,638 | 3,553 | 31,634 | 1,416 | 22.34 |

| 5wI | 10wM |
|-----|------|
| 88 | 14 |

**Career Best Performances:**
167 v. Nottinghamshire, Trent Bridge, 1936
33.4-15-34-9 v. Yorkshire, Bramall Lane, Sheffield, 1934

James Langridge, who was always known as Jim in Sussex, had the misfortune to be an almost exact contemporary of the great Yorkshire slow left-arm bowler, Hedley Verity. Had this not been so, he might well have won more than the eight Test caps that came his way. His and his brother John's upbringing in the village of Newick in the Sussex Weald was filled with the joys of cricket. They played for their school in county tournaments and were supported by Mr Baden-Powell, a cousin of the Chief Scout. Jim suffered from tuberculosis as a boy and, when he collapsed in a game at Ringmer, Baden-Powell arranged for him to be accompanied by Ted Bowley on a recuperative holiday when the Sussex professional went on a coaching trip to New Zealand.

Jim joined the County in 1924, but did not command a regular place until the 1927 season. He was seen at that time to be a correct left-hand batsman: the unmistakable stamp of the good batsman was implicit in strokes played without hurry. In his first full season he missed his 1,000 runs by 8 and his maiden century by 4, but in the following season he was able to reach both these targets. He now sought to develop his bowling, but initially proved expensive by trying to spin the ball too much. In 1929, however, he took 81 wickets at 21 each and, at the beginning of the 1930s, although his batting was not quite living up to expectations, he had become one of the best bowlers of his kind. At his best, he was a genuine slow bowler who employed slight, but extremely skilful, variations of flight. In 1932, *Wisden* made him one of its cricketers of the year and in that season he took 7 Gloucestershire wickets for 8 runs at Cheltenham. It was not surprising, therefore, that he played two Tests for England against the West Indies in 1933 and had an analysis of 7 for 56 in the visitors' second innings at Old Trafford, where one of his scalps was the redoubtable George Headley. He toured India in 1933/34 and played in the three Test matches, and in 1934, in the course of 33.4 overs, he took 9 Yorkshire wickets for 34 at Sheffield.

Jim was becoming one of England's top all-rounders, but, although he went on MCC tours with E.R.T. Holmes' side to Australasia in 1935/36 and with Lord Tennyson's touring party to India in 1937/38, he failed to be included in the England side against Australia in

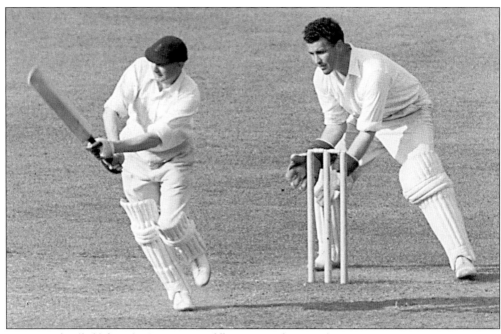

*Jim Langridge* (left) *bats for Sussex v. Middlesex at Lord's in 1953.*

1934 or 1938. Indeed, he only played for England on two further occasions before the advent of the Second World War. Although he was an infinitely better batsman than Hedley Verity, the Yorkshireman edged him out of the bowling department for England at a time when it could be said that the strength of England's upper order rarely needed bolstering from all-rounders.

After service in the NFS during the Second World War, Jim found himself in 1946 a major, if somewhat older, all-rounder in English cricket. The sad death of Hedley Verity in Italy in 1943 left a gap to be filled by a top-class slow left-arm bowler and Jim found himself recalled for the Third Test against India in 1946 and selected for the 1946/47 tour of Australasia under Walter Hammond's captaincy. By this time he was forty and he did not immediately make much impact. After the Third Test, however, he batted well and reached his hundred against South Australia and was set to be included in the side for the Fourth Test. Unfortunately, a groin injury from a previous match was aggravated and he was unable to take any further part in the tour. His ambition to play against Australia, therefore, remained unfulfilled.

Jim continued to play county cricket, bolstering both the Sussex batting and bowling and taking part with George Cox in 1949 in an unbroken fourth wicket stand of 326, which remains a County record for that wicket. In 1950, after one of Sussex's stormy general meetings and Hugh Bartlett's resignation as skipper, Jim was appointed the County's first professional captain. It is possible that he felt that this appointment ended the line to which he belonged – that of the great south country professional cricketers. Nevertheless, he carried out the duties with characteristically unassuming wisdom and courtesy until 1952, when he handed over to David Sheppard. After one more season, in which he headed the national first-class batting averages, he retired to become county coach, but was abruptly dismissed in 1959. Jim's son, Richard, believes that he was so saddened by this event that it may have hastened his relatively early death from cancer just after his sixtieth birthday in 1966. But Jim Langridge's memory remains: one of the truly great Sussex all-rounders, comparable to Maurice Tate and Albert Relf.

# John G. Langridge MBE

*RHB & RM, 1928-55*

**Born:** Chailey, 10 February 1910
**Died:** Eastbourne, 27 June 1999

**County Cap:** 1933

**Batting Record:**

| M | I | NO | Runs | Avge |
|---|---|----|------|------|
| 567 | 972 | 66 | 34,152 | 37.69 |
| **100** | **50** | | **CT/ST** | |
| 76 | 155 | | 776 | |

**Bowling Record:**

| O | M | Runs | W | Avge |
|---|---|------|---|------|
| 544 | 82 | 1,848 | 44 | 42.00 |

**Career Best Performances:**
250* v. Glamorgan, Hove, 1933
7-3-15-3 v. Nottinghamshire, Trent Bridge, 1937

John Langridge was perhaps the best opening batsman never to have played for England, nor has any player with over 34,000 first-class runs and 76 hundreds to his name ever failed to win a Test cap, but that, sadly, was John's fate. His early life was full of cricket: his father played for the Chailey club in the Sussex Weald and his elder brother James had joined the Sussex staff in 1924. He played his first match for Sussex in 1928 and his batting, built on sound principles, correct rather than graceful, with an open stance but ever watchful and yet not lacking in strokes, soon came to be recognised. He was an admirable player of fast bowling, happier against it than when playing spin: in short, he made the ideal opening batsman.

John made a relatively slow start to his career, but by 1932 he was fortunate to find himself in some opening partnerships with Ted Bowley, an accomplished stroke-maker and the rock of the Sussex batting in the twenties and early thirties. In 1933, they enjoyed an opening of partnership of 490 against Middlesex at Hove, Ted eventually making 283, while John's own share was 195. A member in the pavilion, while congratulating him on his innings, added: 'But you were a bit slow, John!' In fact, Ted and John had been together for only five hours and fifty minutes and their opening partnership remains the fourth highest in first-class cricket.

He passed 1,000 runs in a season 17 times, scoring 2,000 in 11 of them, never 'bagging a pair', and of his 76 centuries eight were doubles, the highest being 250 not out against Glamorgan at Hove in 1933. As the 1930s wore on, he became noticed more and more, *The Times* correspondent commenting: 'His batting is as idiosyncratic as it is stoical.' He became not only one of the game's great accumulators, but also one of the great fidgeters, adjusting every part of his equipment before each ball, a ritual that was never omitted. When, in 1932, Duleepsinhji found that his slip catching ability had deserted him, John was summoned to replace him and he became a first slip *par excellence*, taking over 50 catches in a season on four occasions, 69 being the highest, in 1955 when he was forty-five. 133 of these slip catches were taken off the bowling of his brother, James, and the entry of 'c John Langridge b Jas Langridge' often required the use of a second line in *Wisden* and the sports pages of the national papers. His form throughout the 1930s was such that he was selected for the MCC side to tour India in 1939/40 under his County Captain, 'Jack' Holmes, and with two Sussex colleagues, Billy Griffith and Hugh Bartlett. Sadly, the Second World War intervened and aborted the tour.

Left: *John Langridge* (right) *is seen opening the Sussex innings with David Sheppard at Hove.* Right: *The cartoon depicts John's many opening partners.*

His chance to become an England player – for, surely, he would have played some Tests on the flat Indian pitches – had passed him by.

In 1946, John, after fire service during the war, resumed his county career with Sussex, opening with Jim Parks' younger brother, Harry. Later he formed further successful partnerships with Don Smith and David Sheppard. Excluding his record partnership with Ted Bowley, he was involved in 16 partnerships of over 200 and in one of 307 for the second wicket in 1939 with Harry Parks against Kent at Tonbridge. He was also part of 145 partnerships of over 100 runs, 66 of them for the first wicket. John completed a 'full set' of hundreds against every first-class county, except Warwickshire, and was particularly severe on Derbyshire against whom, between 1949 and 1951, he scored 1,062 runs at an average of 151.7. Of this total, 526 runs came in 1949 when he made 234 not out in June at Ilkeston and followed a month later with 146 run out and 146 not out at

Worthing. The 1949 season, when he was in his fortieth year, proved to be a record-breaking year as he totalled 2,914 runs (average 60.70) and scored 12 hundreds.

After he retired in 1955, John became a first-class umpire for 25 seasons and, ironically, made it seven times on to the Test arena in this capacity. *Wisden* observed that, in this new phase of his life, 'his concentration, his affability and his quiet, but old-fashioned insistence on standards made him universally respected.' In 1978, he was appointed MBE and the TCCB marked his fifty years of service with the presentation of a cheque and a silver coffee pot. He still holds four of the five Sussex batting records: most runs in a season 2,850 (average 64.77); most runs in a career 34,152 (average 37.69); most hundreds in a season 12; and most hundreds in a career 76. Few players at any time in the history of the sport can have made a greater contribution to cricket than John Langridge.

# Richard J. Langridge
*LHB & OB, 1957-71*

**Born:** Brighton, 13 April 1939

**County Cap:** 1961

**Batting Record:**

| M | I | NO | Runs | Avge |
|---|---|----|------|------|
| 207 | 383 | 28 | 8,143 | 22.93 |
| *29* | *27* | *2* | *486* | *19.44* |

| 100 | 50 | | CT/ST |
|-----|----|--|-------|
| 5 | 40 | | 186 |
| - | *2* | | *14* |

**Bowling Record:**

| O | M | Runs | W | Avge |
|---|---|------|---|------|
| 14 | 3 | 81 | 0 | -- |

| 5wI | 10wM |
|-----|------|
| - | - |
| - | - |

**Career Best Performances:**
137* v. Leicestershire, Leicester, 1963
*74 v. Hampshire, Hove, 1970 (SL)*

If you were born into a family where talk rarely deviated from Sussex cricket and Brighton football, it could be difficult not to follow the family tradition, but this was largely the fate of Richard Langridge. His father, James, and uncle John were, of course, the best of men – Sussex can rarely have had such devoted cricketers – but Richard felt that any other course was inconceivable. 'Dad would have been terribly disappointed', he said later. At Brighton and Hove Grammar School, Richard showed no particular aptitude for cricket and his headmaster advised him to train for a career 'with predictable rewards', but nevertheless, at the age of eighteen, he made his debut for the County, did little in that season and the next and then fulfilled his National Service.

Richard's real career with the County began in 1961, when he started to open the innings, totalled 1,675 runs in all matches with two hundreds and was awarded his county cap. In the following season he went one better with 1,885 runs, 41 catches at short-leg and the media talking about his England prospects. But things did not work out for this modest and thoughtful man: he recognised that he was largely a front-foot player and did not have the strength to play powerfully off the back foot. The canny pros noticed it too – 'before long I did not get anything pitched up'. Scoring slowly did not please some members of the crowd either, although, ironically perhaps, he did have some success in Sussex's two wins in the inaugural years of the Gillette Cup. In 1963 his half century against Yorkshire and his solid 34 in an opening partnership with Alan Oakman in the final were certainly integral parts of the County's success.

After the 1965 season, Richard asked the County for time off to train as a teacher and, although he returned to play a full season in 1970, his heart was not in it. 'When I found I was playing fourteen days' non-stop cricket, I just did not enjoy it any more.' So, after the odd game for the County in 1971, he retired and devoted himself to teaching. While he trained he spent some time in South Africa, met his wife there and at Queenstown taught Tony Greig, whom he recommended to the County. He has now found his niche in life, but he did play his part for the County.

# George Leach
*RHB & RF, 1903-14*

**Born:** Malta, 18 July 1881
**Died:** Rawntenstall, Lancashire, 10 January 1945

**Batting Record:**

| M | I | NO | Runs | Avge |
|---|---|----|------|------|
| 225 | 350 | 42 | 5,788 | 18.79 |
| **100** | **50** | | **CT/ST** | |
| 2 | 22 | | 106 | |

**Bowling Record:**

| O | M | Runs | W | Avge |
|---|---|------|---|------|
| 3,472 | 629 | 11,528 | 413 | 27.91 |
| **5wI** | **10wM** | | | |
| 19 | 1 | | | |

**Career Best Performances:**
113* v. Derbyshire, Hove, 1909
23.3-6-48-8 v. Lancashire, Old Trafford, 1909

George Leach, a hard-hitting batsman and fast bowler, joined Sussex in 1903, but did not make his mark until the following season, when he made over 500 runs. He scored a maiden century – 106 versus Essex at Leyton – in 1905 and in the following year reached 1,016 runs and took 47 wickets in all matches. Although he took over 50 wickets in 1907, it was not until two years later that he passed 100 wickets in a season. He continued to contribute with both bat and ball until 1911, but after that season his appearances became more sporadic and he gave up first-class cricket in 1914. He then moved to north and played his cricket in the Lancashire leagues.

George did not have a fixed place in the Sussex batting order and batted almost everywhere between opener and number 11, although he was generally to be found in the late middle order. Against Derbyshire at Hove in 1909, batting at number eight, he made 113 not out and, together with his captain, Charles Smith, who made 66 not out, added an unbroken 179 in 80 minutes. In the following season, when the County were forced to follow on against Warwickshire at Leamington, he was involved with John Vincett in a partnership of 126 in 50 minutes which, according to *Wisden* involved 'some brilliant hitting and not only averted defeat but also brought about a highly creditable draw.' As a bowler, he took 8 wickets in an innings on three occasions: 8 for 150 versus Surrey at Hove in 1908, together with 8 for 48 versus Lancashire at Old Trafford and 8 for 61 versus Warwickshire at Edgbaston, both in 1909, his season of great bowling success. His most impressive performance, however, was his 7 for 26 against Middlesex at Lord's in 1909 when he and Albert Relf dismissed the London side for 47. George, again according to the *Wisden* report, 'made the ball break back surprisingly for so fast a bowler.'

George was certainly an accomplished sportsman and he enjoyed a good career in association football. Described as a massive old-style centre-forward, he helped Eastbourne win the Sussex Senior Cup in 1899 and later, while playing for Eastbourne and then Hailsham, represented Sussex. In 1904, he was with Brighton and Hove Albion before moving to Tottenham Hotspur. His itinerant career took him then to Tunbridge Wells Rangers before he returned to the Goldstone in 1909.

**Born:** Lancing, 24 May 1936

**County Cap:** 1957

**Batting Record:**

| M | I | NO | Runs | Avge |
|---|---|---|---|---|
| 300 | 539 | 50 | 12,796 | 26.16 |
| *21* | *20* | *1* | *370* | *19.47* |
| **100** | **50** | | **CT/ST** | |
| 7 | 65 | | 110 | |
| - | *1* | | *4* | |

**Bowling Record:**

| O | M | Runs | W | Avge |
|---|---|---|---|---|
| 90 | 23 | 306 | 6 | 51.00 |
| **5wI** | **10wM** | | | |
| - | - | | | |
| - | - | | | |

**Career Best Performances:**
191* v. Warwickshire, Edgbaston, 1963
*70 v. Nottinghamshire, Trent Bridge, 1969 (SL)*
6-1-24-2 v. Nottinghamshire, Eastbourne, 1962

At the start of his career with the County, Les Lenham was seen as 'a Sussex opening batsman of the future and a classy one at that'. He did not perhaps wholly fulfil this prediction, but over fifteen seasons he made a strong contribution to Sussex's fortunes, especially in the first half of his career. Les hailed from Worthing and was educated at the high school there. He became associated with the County as early as 1952, but did not make his debut until 1956, after he had completed his National Service.

In 1957, his first full season, he was given his head as an opener and was an immediate success, scoring over 1,400 runs, a maiden century and carrying his bat through the County's innings (66 out of 147) against Surrey. For the next few seasons, he was mainly at the top of the batting order and 1963 was the fifth season where he had scored over 1,000 runs. In 1960 he again batted through an innings, making 51 out of 161 against Glamorgan in a knock which *Wisden* praised for 'his concentration over four hours on a difficult pitch.' The following season, however, was undoubtedly his best, as he reached 2,000 runs in 35 matches and 68 innings, including a hundred before lunch in the Middlesex match at Hove, while in the next two seasons he managed to make exactly the same number of runs – 1,334 – in each of them. The latter season also produced his highest score, 191 not out against Warwickshire where he batted, unusually at number four, for five-and-a-half hours and hit 2 sixes and 25 fours. From then on his career dipped a little. Although he again passed 1,000 runs in 1966, his contribution became markedly less substantial and in 1970 he retired from the first-class game, having played mainly for the Second XI in his latter years and after captaining the side jointly with Richard Langridge in 1969.

His precise, almost classical, style of batting was not perhaps suited to the limited-overs game, but in the County's first two successful years in the Gillette Cup he played a full part, usually in the middle order and scoring valuable runs.

On his retirement, Les became the County's coach for a few seasons before becoming the National Cricket Association's chief regional coach in 1974, a post in which he became renowned for his skill. Nowadays, he is still happy to impart his coaching skills to aspiring young cricketers.

# Neil J. Lenham
*RHB & RM, 1984-97*

**Born:** Worthing, 17 December 1965

**County Cap:** 1990

**Batting Record:**

| M | I | NO | Runs | Avge |
|---|---|---|---|---|
| 192 | 332 | 29 | 10,135 | 33.44 |
| *141* | *125* | *26* | *3,052* | *30.83* |

| 100 | 50 | | CT/ST | |
|---|---|---|---|---|
| 20 | 49 | | 73 | |
| *1* | *18* | | *23* | |

**Bowling Record:**

| O | M | Runs | W | Avge |
|---|---|---|---|---|
| 606 | 118 | 1,847 | 42 | 43.97 |
| *261.3* | *5* | *1,347* | *44* | *30.61* |

**Career Best Performances:**
222* v. Kent, Hove, 1992
*129* v. Devon, Hove, 1995 (NWT)*
15-9-13-4 v. Durham, Durham University 1993
*10-0-28-5 v. Durham, Durham University, 1993 (SL)*

Fame at an early age can sometimes be impossible to live up to. When he left Brighton College at the end of the 1984 season, Neil Lenham was hailed by the *Cricketer* as 'one of the brightest school prospects since the war.' This was certainly no exaggeration, as he had broken just about every record in the book. His performance had been phenomenal: 42 centuries in all cricket, a record 1,534 runs (average 80.74) in the 1984 season, 4,084 runs overall for his school's First XI, 50 wickets for peanuts in his last year and one of the few schoolboy cricketers to score a double ton. Even more demanding was a constant suggestion in the media that he would reach the very top.

Neil did not, in fact, achieve all that was perhaps hoped for him, although his technique as an opening batsman, honed by his father Les, was absolutely first-class. His early years at Sussex did not bring forth the expected results, although he made his maiden hundred, 104 not out, against the Pakistanis in 1987. It was not until 1990 that his potential started to come through, and he then topped the Championship averages and made over 1,600 runs in all matches. This proved to be his best season, although he passed 1,000 runs in the next two

and in 1992 he made his highest score, 222 not out, against Kent at Hove in a contrived match. *Wisden* was quite scathing, referring to Kent's 'sending down 75 ludicrous overs' and adding that there had been 'far worthier centuries' than Neil's. A much better innings had been his 193 against Leicestershire at Hove in 1991 when, with 26 fours, he made the highest Championship score by a Sussex batsman for seven years. From 1992 onwards, Neil's career tailed off. He never made 1,000 runs again, but he did make some serious contributions to limited-overs matches, where early on he had not achieved greatly. His opening batsman's technique did not fit easily into the middle order, but in 1993 his 47 was decisive in helping Alan Wells defeat Glamorgan in the NatWest semi-final.

Neil probably suffered more than his fair share of injuries. Although he continued to make runs in both first-class and limited-overs matches, his appearances were restricted and at the end of the 1997 season he called it a day. Fortunately, the post of marketing manager was there for the taking and he continues to occupy that position today.

# Garth S. le Roux

*RHB & RF, 1978-87*

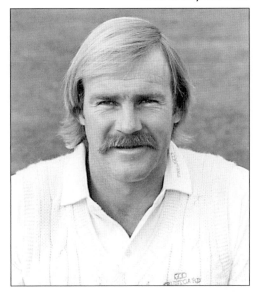

**Born:** Kenilworth, Cape Town, South Africa, 4 September 1955

**County Cap:** 1981

**Batting Record:**

| M | I | NO | Runs | Avge |
|---|---|---|---|---|
| 137 | 156 | 39 | 3,341 | 28.55 |
| *137* | *106* | *26* | *1,997* | *24.96* |

| 100 | 50 | | CT/ST |
|---|---|---|---|
| - | 18 | | 38 |
| - | *8* | | *28* |

**Bowling Record:**

| O | M | Runs | W | Avge |
|---|---|---|---|---|
| 3,277 | 778 | 9,114 | 393 | 23.19 |
| *1,050* | *88* | *4,065* | *196* | *20.74* |

| 5wI | 10wM |
|---|---|
| 15 | 1 |
| *2* | *-* |

**Career Best Performances:**
83 v. Surrey, Hove, 1982
*88 v. Glamorgan, Hastings, 1982 (SL)*
33.2-10-107-8 v. Somerset, Taunton, 1981
*7-4-7-5 v. Ireland, Hove, 1985 (NWT)*

Garth le Roux would almost certainly have enjoyed a successful Test match career but for South Africa's long exclusion from international cricket. As it was, county cricket with Sussex, provincial cricket in South Africa and a flirtation with Kerry Packer's World Series Cricket was all that came the way of this genuinely fast bowler.

The son of a merchant navy captain, he was born in the Cape and attended Wynberg Boys' High School and Stellenbosch University, where he obtained a BA in Physical Education. After school and university he made a spectacular entrance into South African cricket when he took 53 wickets in only 8 Currie Cup matches in 1975/76. In 1977, his South African colleague, Eddie Barlow, persuaded him to try county cricket with Derbyshire and this was followed by a trial for Sussex, for whom he played one match – against the New Zealanders – in the following year. After some procrastination all round, he finally signed for Sussex and the TCCB cleared him to play in 1980.

With his huge frame and great strength, Garth was an immediate success. For the next eight seasons he was an integral part of the County team, scoring a substantial number of runs in the middle order – 737 (average 32.04) in 1982 his best performance – and taking a significant number of wickets each year. In 1981, he took 81 wickets (average 19.53) and with Imran Khan (who took 66 wickets) formed what was undoubtedly the best opening attack on the county circuit. What with Paul Parker's excellent batting and John Barclay's astute captaincy, it was not surprising that Sussex reached second place in the County Championship, something that they had not achieved since 1953. Garth and Imran also played a leading part in the County's success, both when they won the John Player Sunday League in 1982 and also when they lifted the NatWest Trophy in 1986.

In 1987 he was plagued by injury and decided to call it a day, but not before he had left Sussex supporters with something to remember. His 83 not out against Hampshire in the Sunday League match at Horsham was made from 54 balls and, when the County needed 5 runs from the last ball, he hit it for the sixth of his sixes in the match. No wonder he ended the season with 354 runs (average 70.80) in this competition. It was certainly something to go away with.

69

# Jason D. Lewry

*LHB & LFM, 1994-*

**Born:** Worthing, 2 April 1971

**County Cap: 1996**

**Batting Record:**

| M | I | NO | Runs | Avge |
|---|---|---|---|---|
| 88 | 122 | 23 | 948 | 9.58 |
| *51* | *30* | *11* | *147* | *7.74* |
| 100 | 50 | | CT/ST | |
| - | - | | 16 | |
| - | - | | 4 | |

**Bowling Record:**

| O | M | Runs | W | Avge |
|---|---|---|---|---|
| 2,602 | 590 | 8,282 | 322 | 25.72 |
| *419.4* | *21* | *1,655* | *69* | *23.99* |
| 5wI | 10wM | | | |
| 20 | 3 | | | |
| - | - | | | |

**Career Best Performances:**
47 v. Gloucestershire, Hove, 2001
*16 v. Lancashire, Old Trafford, 2001 (C&G)*
12.1-3-38-7 v. Derbyshire, Derby, 1999
*7.1-0-29-4 v. Somerset, Bath, 1995 (SL)*

Sniffed out by Sussex scouts in 1993 from the Goring Club, Jason Lewry made his debut in 1994 and one season later he was bowling over 300 overs, taking 47 wickets and topping the County's Championship bowling averages. It was certainly fast-track stuff. In the next season, he again topped the County bowling averages and was rated by Sussex coach, Desmond Haynes, as one of the best swing bowlers in the country and a possible candidate for international honours. Jason then, however, encountered a setback. The injury that can strike quick bowlers caught up with him and he spent the whole of the following season undergoing surgery to his lower back and playing no cricket at all.

By 1998, however, Jason and James Kirtley had formed one of the best opening attacks in the country. Jason's tally was 62 wickets (average 22.72) and, as a result, he found himself selected for the England 'A' party visiting Zimbabwe and South Africa in the winter of 1998/99. Sadly, the tour did not live up to his expectations. He had begun the tour with a slight knee problem, but, having overcome that, he went down with a bout of food poisoning and was then forced to return home with a shoulder injury. These setbacks did not dim his enthu-

siasm and, although he missed the first seven weeks of the next season, he came back strongly with 56 wickets (average 23.75), including a match-winning 7 wickets for 38 – 10 in the match – against Derbyshire. In the following two seasons, he remained in harness with James and took over 50 wickets in both years. Sussex's neighbours, Hampshire, felt the effects of his skill at Hove in July 2001. After taking 6 for 37 in the visitors' first innings, he totally demolished their second attempt by beginning with a hat-trick, taking 5 wickets in 7 balls, 6 in 10 balls and 7 in 13 balls – this is something that only Pat Pocock (Surrey) with 7 wickets in 11 balls has surpassed in county cricket. He ended with 7 for 42 and 13 for 79 in the match.

Quite without peer when sultry conditions prevail, he produces remarkably late in-swing with the new ball, as a glance at scorebooks, often showing openers bowled or trapped lbw by him in the first over, will indicate. How he has missed Test match honours is a mystery, as is the committee's reluctance to use such a jewel more often in limited-overs matches.

# Frederick William Lillywhite

*RHB & SRA, 1825-53*

**Born:** Westhampnett, 13 June 1792
**Died:** Islington, Middlesex, 21 August 1854

**Batting Record:**

| M | I | NO | Runs | Avge |
|---|---|----|------|------|
| 74 | 135 | 22 | 745 | 6.59 |

| 50 | 100 | | CT/ST |
|----|-----|--|-------|
| - | - | | 43 |

**Bowling Record:**

| Runs | W | Avge | Other wickets |
|------|---|------|---------------|
| 564 | 49 | 11.51 | 425 |

| 5wI | 10wM (including 'other | |
|-----|------------------------|--|
| 37 | 12 | wickets') |

**Career Best Performances:**
42* v. MCC, Lord's, 1839
9-29 v. Hants and Surrey, Bramshill, 1826

Much information about William Lillywhite has been lost in the mists of time, although it is certainly true that he was known as 'Old Lilly' – to distinguish him from later members of the famous family. His father ran the Duke of Richmond's brickyards at Goodwood and he himself learned the trade there. In 1822, he came to Brighton and took charge of a brickfield at Hove and, although there is no evidence whether he played cricket before he was about thirty, he first played for Sussex in 1825. He was a determined little man, only 5ft 4in tall, who always wore a black, broad-brimmed hat. He is believed to have introduced round-arm bowling in conjunction with Jem Broadbridge, possibly because an injury to his arm made bowling underarm difficult and despite opposition from many cricketers who found this method unfair. How many wickets he took is difficult to register as catches and stumpings were then not usually credited to the bowler. In 1826, he took 16 wickets for Sussex against a Surrey and Hampshire team and twelve years later he managed 14 wickets against England. Stories of his complacency abound. He once said: 'I suppose if I thought every ball, they would never get a run' and, on another occasion, he defined cricket at its best

as 'Pilch (of Kent) batting, me bowling and Box keeping wicket.' He is once believed to have bowled 60 balls to Fuller Pilch without a run being scored and to have bowled him with the sixty-first. Certainly, the 49 wickets officially credited to him in Sussex records are far fewer than those he actually took and it is believed that he took at least another 425. Over the whole of his first-class career, he probably took some 1,355 wickets.

In 1837, he took the lease of the Sovereign Inn in Preston Street and acquired the Temple Fields cricket ground, now the site of Montpelier Square, where he would bowl to members with a long-stop, often someone like John Wisden. In 1844, he was in dispute over leases and moved to London and joined MCC as a bowler. He stayed there until his death, although between 1851 and 1853 he coached at Winchester College. After he died of cholera at Islington in 1854, he was buried in Highgate Cemetery and MCC members erected a headstone which paid tribute to his reputation, character and 'teaching by precept and example.'

# James Lillywhite junior
*LHB & SMLA, 1862-83*

**Born:** Westhampnett, 23 February 1842
**Died:** Westerton, Chichester, 25 October 1929

**Batting Record:**

| M | I | NO | Runs | Avge |
|---|---|----|------|------|
| 157 | 277 | 33 | 3,627 | 14.86 |
| **100** | **50** | | **CT/ST** | |
| 2 | 10 | | 68 | |

**Bowling Career:**

| Runs | W | Avge |
|------|---|------|
| 12,862 | 855 | 15.04 |
| **5wI** | **10wM** | |
| 76 | 18 | |

**Career Best Performances:**
126* v. Middlesex, at the Old Cattle Market Ground, Islington, 1868
9-29 v. MCC, Lord's 1862

James Lillywhite junior (to distinguish him from his cousin) was the son of John Lillywhite, the younger brother of William Lillywhite, the *nonpareil* bowler. His cricketing cousins were James senior, John and Frederick, the three sons of William. He made his debut for Sussex in 1862 versus MCC and Ground at Lord's, taking 5 for 28 in the first innings and 9 for 29 in the second and bowling unchanged throughout the match – he did so on a further eleven occasions, including three times in consecutive matches in 1873. In the next year, he repeated the feat with 9 for 73 against Kent at Sandgate. His capacity for cricket was legendary and from 1862 to 1881 he played in every single Sussex match. At the start of his career, he showed promise as a hard-hitting left-handed batsman, but as his skill as a bowler increased, his batting waned. Exceptionally accurate and with an easy round-arm action, he was a left-hand bowler who pioneered the tactics of keeping the ball on the off-side and cutting it away from the right-handed batsman. He was also an excellent fielder at either slip or mid-on.

James visited Australia on six occasions, the first in 1873/74 under Dr W.G. Grace and the next in 1876/77, when he himself led the team and played the first two official Test matches against Australia, which resulted in one win for each side. He was, therefore, England's first Test captain. His other four visits 'Down Under' were in business partnership with Alfred Shaw and Arthur Shrewsbury. Prior to this, he had been a member of E. Willsher's team to the United States and Canada in 1868 and, later on, he was responsible for the fixture lists of the first two Australian teams which visited England in 1878 and 1880.

As a cricketer, he was reputed to be imperturbable, cheerful and self-possessed and, although he suffered more than most bowlers from dropped catches, he never showed annoyance. This placid temperament probably led to his being selected for umpiring duties. He was a Test umpire before he played his last first-class game, officiating in all four Tests against Australia in Sydney and Melbourne in 1881/82. He stood again in the Second Test of the 1884/85 series, but only once in England, officiating in the Fourth Test against Australia at Old Trafford in 1899, when Arthur Hide, another former Sussex player, stood at the other end.

# Arnold Long
*LHB & WK, 1976-80*

**Born:** Cheam, Surrey, 18 December 1940

**County Cap:** 1976
**County Captain:** 1978-1980

**Batting Record:**

| M | I | NO | Runs | Avge |
|---|---|----|------|------|
| 97 | 123 | 40 | 1,689 | 20.35 |
| *104* | *59* | *14* | *435* | *9.89* |

| 100 | 50 | CT/ST | |
|-----|----|-------|--|
| - | 2 | 216/21 | |
| - | - | *101/12* | |

**Bowling Record:**

| O | M | Runs | W | Avge |
|---|---|------|---|------|
| 1 | 0 | 2 | 0 | - |

| 5wI | 10wM |
|-----|------|
| - | - |

**Career Best Performances:**
60 v. Hampshire, Basingstoke, 1976
*33 v. Surrey, The Oval, 1978 (SL)*
Best season, 1976: (71 dismissals, 63ct, 8st)

Arnold Long enjoyed a lengthy career with Surrey before he came to Sussex in 1976. He first played at the Oval as an eighteen-year-old on leaving Wallington County Grammar School and became their regular 'keeper in 1962. Two years later, he set a new world record, now equalled by five other 'keepers, when he caught 11 batsmen in the match against Sussex at Hove. His style was effective rather than ostentatious and his ability to lead on the field was rewarded by the Surrey vice-captaincy in 1973.

When Lonsdale Skinner, a better batsman, edged Arnold out from behind the stumps at the Oval, he moved in 1976 to Sussex where Alan Mansell had not made the grade. His first two seasons showed his technically sound wicket-keeping at its best and 71 dismissals in his first season proved his worth. In 1977, Sussex were going through a bad patch: Tony Greig, the captain, played only half the first-class matches and was preoccupied with Kerry Packer's circus. Team morale was low and so for the 1978 season the Committee opted for Arnold as skipper. His task was not an easy one, but *Wisden* succinctly summed up his performance: 'Wicketkeeper

Long, so different from Greig in temperament, persevered in a cool and admirable fashion, steadily rebuilding the old team spirit and reaping a thrilling reward when he was hoisted on the shoulders of his team-mates, with the Gillette Cup raised aloft, on the balcony at Lord's.' He was not, of course, a star, but he was an admirable and efficient manager of a cricket team and in this manner he brought the County through to its third limited-overs Cup Final success. The attack restrained the power of Somerset's batting duo, Viv Richards and Ian Botham, and, when Paul Parker's batting guided the County home, the crowd's enthusiastic applause was testament to his skill as a leader.

In the following year, Sussex reached the semi-final of the Gillette Cup, but were denied by Allan Lamb's hundred. In the County Championship, however, Arnold led the County to fourth place, something that had not been equalled since the heady days of Ted Dexter's leadership in 1963. He played on as skipper for one further season, sometimes dropping out of the team to allow younger players to gain experience, and he then handed over to John Barclay for the 1981 season. As *Wisden* again so perceptively observed: 'Long's thoughtful captaincy served Sussex well.'

# Robin G. Marlar

*RHB & OB, 1951-68*

Born: Eastbourne, 2 January 1931

County Cap: 1952
County Captain: 1955-1959
Chairman: 1997-1999

Batting Record:

| M | I | NO | Runs | Avge |
|---|---|----|------|------|
| 223 | 303 | 50 | 2,576 | 10.18 |
| 100 | 50 | | CT/ST | |
| - | 2 | | 110 | |

Bowling Record:

| O | M | Runs | W | Avge |
|---|---|------|---|------|
| 6,725 | 1,859 | 17,918 | 740 | 24.21 |
| 5wI | 10wM | | | |
| 52 | 10 | | | |

Career Best Performances:
64 v. Australians, Hove, 1956
23.2-8-46-9 v. Lancashire, Hove, 1955

Educated at Harrow and Cambridge University, Robin Marlar first played for Sussex in 1951 during his first year at university. In the following season he took 108 wickets, 56 of them for the County, and established himself as an important off-spinner in English cricket. A year later he captained Cambridge and during the season bowled over 1,300 overs – only Johnny Wardle of Yorkshire bowled more – and took 136 wickets, including another 56 for Sussex, 12 in the Varsity match and 7 for 79 for the Gentlemen in the Players' second innings.

On leaving Cambridge he began playing full-time for Sussex, although in 1954 only 61 of his 86 wickets were for Sussex, as he was often in demand for the Gentlemen and MCC sides. When Hubert Doggart decided to return to teaching at the end of the 1954 season, Marlar was invited to take on the leadership for 1955, remaining in post until the end of the 1959 when he handed over to Ted Dexter. His first year was eminently successful and Sussex finished in fourth place in the Championship, although they were subsequently less successful.

It was Robin's misfortune to be playing at a time when Jim Laker was at the height of his powers and he was doubtless unlucky not to

have won a Test cap, as he was certainly the best amateur spinner of his time – witness the eight consecutive appearances he made for the Gentlemen at Lord's between 1951 and 1958. Some other performances were outstanding – 15 wickets for 119 runs, including 9 for 46 against Lancashire at Hove in 1955, and 15 for 133 against Glamorgan at Swansea in 1952. The latter match formed part of a remarkable performance, when between 23 and 29 August he bowled 126.4 overs, 46 maidens and took 27 wickets for 268 runs at an average of 9.93, Lancashire joining Glamorgan as his victims. He was not a great batsman, but his 64 off the touring Australians, with 5 sixes and 6 fours, in 1956 must have been well worth watching.

Although Robin played some games in 1960, he had decided to move into other spheres. He contested Bolsover in the 1959 General Election but, unsurprisingly, Harrow and Cambridge did not go down too well with that mining community and so he went into journalism, writing frequently for the *Sunday Times* and elsewhere. When Sussex suffered its 1997 upheaval, he stepped in as chairman for two years and saw the County through into smoother waters.

# Alan Melville
## *RHB & LBG, 1932-36*

**Born:** Carnarvon, Cape Province, South Africa, 19 May 1910
**Died:** Sabie, Transvaal, South Africa, 18 April 1983

**County Captain:** 1934-1935

**Batting Record:**

| M | I | NO | Runs | Avge |
|---|---|----|------|------|
| 86 | 132 | 7 | 4,952 | 39.61 |
| 100 | 50 | | CT/ST | |
| 12 | 26 | | 65 | |

**Bowling Record:**

| O | M | Runs | W | Avge |
|---|---|------|---|------|
| 353 | 35 | 1,365 | 38 | 35.92 |
| 5wI | 10wM | | | |
| 2 | - | | | |

**Career Best Performances:**
152 v. Indians, Hove, 1936
5.3-0-17-5 v. Gloucestershire, Gloucester, 1933

Aged seventeen and still at Michaelhouse School in South Africa, Alan Melville was picked for Natal, and in the following season he scored a hundred in the trial match to select the national side to tour England in 1929. His father, however, decided that, as Alan was coming to England to take his place at Oxford University, it would be better to refuse. In 1930, having scored a hundred and taken 8 wickets in the Freshmen's match, he adapted easily to playing on grass, scored a hundred against Yorkshire and gained the first of his four blues. When the Oxford captain fell ill in 1931, he took over the reins and captained the university in his own right in 1932.

In 1932, Alan started playing for Sussex in the university vacations and, after leaving Oxford, captained the County in the 1934 and 1935 seasons. He was arguably the most elegant batsman of his time, a powerful hooker and a driver of consummate ease. In 1933, having just left Oxford, he played for Sussex against the West Indians at Hove. It was the summer following the 'bodyline' series in Australia and the West Indian quicks, Griffith and Martindale, were in full flow. Whatever they served up to Alan, short balls and half-volleys, was dispatched with such conviction that his 114 even put John Langridge's well-crafted 172 into the shade. In his last innings for Sussex in 1936 he made his highest score – 152 against the Indians – and then returned home to take up a position on the Johannesburg Stock Exchange.

But that was not the end of him in cricket. He immediately became captain of the Wanderers, Transvaal's leading club, and when England toured South Africa in 1938/39 he captained his country. In the last match of the series, the famous 'Timeless Test' at Durban, he made 78 and 103 and then the Second World War intervened. In 1947 he was captain of the South Africans in England, and in the First Test at Trent Bridge he made 189 and 104 not out and followed this with 117 at Lord's. He created cricket history by being the first man to score four consecutive Test hundreds against England. His career, however, was now winding down; he played one further Test in 1948 before retiring and becoming a highly respected selector. For Sussex, of course, he was something of a good luck charm; the County were runners-up three times in the Championship in his five years at Hove.

# Gehan D. Mendis

*RHB, RM & WK, 1973-85*

**Born:** Colombo, Sri Lanka, 20 April 1955

**County Cap:** 1980

**Batting Record:**

| M | I | NO | Runs | Avge |
|---|---|---|---|---|
| 202 | 354 | 32 | 11,272 | 35.01 |
| *172* | *168* | *15* | *4,635* | *30.36* |
| **100** | **50** | | **CT/ST** | |
| 22 | 51 | | 89/1 | |
| *6* | *22* | | *52* | |

**Bowling Record:**

| O | M | Runs | W | Avge |
|---|---|---|---|---|
| 6 | 0 | 76 | 1 | 76.00 |
| **5wl** | **10wM** | | | |
| - | - | | | |

**Career Best Performances:**
209* v. Somerset, Hove, 1984
*141* v. Warwickshire, Hove, 1980 (GC)*
4-0-65-1 v. Yorkshire, Hove, 1985

The English-speaking Mendis family, concerned for their children's education, emigrated to this country from Sri Lanka in 1968 when Sinhalese became the main language in schools there. Gehan, the youngest of their three children, joined the Brighton, Hove and Sussex Grammar School and went on to Durham University. He first played for the County in a one-day match in 1973 and made his first-class debut in the following year, but he had to wait until 1977 to gain real first team experience. In 1978, he scored a maiden century against Gloucestershire and totalled over 900 runs in all matches, and in the following seven seasons, now established as a regular opening batsman – a position in which he thrived – he scored over 1,000 runs in six of them, 1,756 (average 47.45) in 1985 being his best return. He must have come very close to England selection. It is possible that his failure to catch the selectors' eye was due to a misunderstanding. In 1980, in a Gillette Cup tie at Hove, he scored 141 not out in a win over Warwickshire and when Alec Bedser, chairman of selectors, presented him with the man of the match award he appeared to think that Gehan had opted to play international cricket for Sri Lanka. This

was some error for a young man's career!

Not only was he an outstanding performer in the first-class game, but he also made his mark in limited-overs cricket, playing an important part in the County's win over Somerset in the 1978 Gillette final and recording an estimable average of over 30 in the short game. In 1985 he became the centre of some controversy. He was enjoying a magnificent summer, having scored two hundreds in the match against Lancashire, another in the second innings against Warwickshire, and yet another in the first innings of the Hampshire game – four tons in five knocks. In the second innings at Portsmouth, he had reached 96 when John Barclay declared the Sussex innings closed. Having faced only 4 balls in the preceding five overs, he felt aggrieved at his skipper's closure and that very night decided to shake the dust of Sussex from his feet. Later he is alleged to have cited social exclusion as another reason for wanting to depart. Whatever the cause, he signed for Lancashire for the next season. The fixture list knows no sentiment and Sussex's first match in 1986 was against Lancashire and Gehan departed early (caught Barclay bowled le Roux) for a duck.

# Richard R. Montgomerie

*RHB & OB, 1999-*

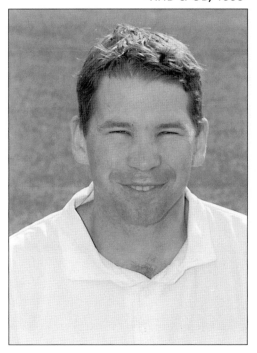

**Born:** Rugby, Warwickshire, 3 July 1971

**County Cap:** 1999

**Batting Record:**

| M | I | NO | Runs | Avge |
|---|---|----|------|------|
| 50 | 90 | 7 | 3,565 | 42.95 |
| *56* | *56* | *6* | *1,921* | *38.42* |
| **100** | **50** | | **CT/ST** | |
| 12 | 15 | | 52 | |
| *1* | *14* | | *10* | |

**Bowling Career:**

| O | M | Runs | W | Avge |
|---|---|------|---|------|
| 7 | 1 | 23 | 1 | 23.00 |
| **5wI** | **10wM** | | | |
| - | - | | | |

**Career Best Performances:**
160* v. Nottinghamshire, Trent Bridge, 2001
*108 v. Essex, Hove, 2001 (SL)*
1-1-0-1 v. Middlesex, Lord's, 2001

One county's misjudgement can sometimes be to another's advantage. When Northamptonshire decided that Richard Montgomerie was surplus to requirements, Sussex must have been delighted. Educated at Rugby School and Oxford University, he gained a blue each year and was University captain in 1994. Making his debut for Northamptonshire in 1991 at the age of nineteen, he showed uneven form, but was occasionally brilliant as, for instance, in his 192 against Kent at Canterbury in 1995. In spite of his occasional flashes of inspiration, he was 'released' – as the modern euphemism goes – at the end of 1998.

When Richard appeared at Hove at the start of the 1999 season, there was an opener's spot awaiting him. The opening pair of Toby Peirce and Wasim Khan had not enjoyed remarkable success in 1998 and it was left to them to battle it out for the one place to accompany Richard. His first season did not quite bring him to 1,000 runs, but he was highly consistent both in the Championship and in limited-overs matches, his average in the latter being over 40. The next season was almost as good as his first, but in 2001 he hit the 'form of his life' as David Gilbert,

Sussex's chief executive at the time, described it. After the departure of the former openers, Richard established a partnership with the Zimbabwe Test batsman, Murray Goodwin, and they hit it off right from the start: 123 together against Hampshire at West End, 212 against Worcestershire at Horsham when they both recorded hundreds, 108 against Middlesex at Lord's and then an imposing 372 for 0 wickets declared against Nottinghamshire at Trent Bridge. Although well below the famous Bowley-Langridge opening stand of 490 against Middlesex in 1933, it was the third highest partnership for any wicket in the County's history. Their dominance was even inflicted on the Australians at Hove in August. Richard scored 157 in a partnership of 202 for the first wicket and the County declared at 355 for 4 wickets off only 91 overs. This was not Australia's Test line-up, but it was a strong side including three regular Test match bowlers and it caused critics to ask whether Richard was in line for an England cap. Sadly, neither a cap nor a touring place for the winter did come his way, but he ended the season with over 1,700 runs, an average of nearly 60 plus 8 hundreds and 5 fifties – certainly the form of his life!

# Peter Moores
*RHB & WK, 1985-98*

**Born:** Macclesfield, Cheshire, 18 December 1962

**County Cap:** 1989
**County Captain:** 1997

**Batting Record:**

| M | I | NO | Runs | Avge |
|---|---|----|------|------|
| 219 | 329 | 40 | 7,086 | 24.51 |
| *231* | *184* | *43* | *2,488* | *17.65* |

| 100 | 50 | | CT/ST | |
|-----|----|--|-------|--|
| 7 | 31 | | 479/38 | |
| - | *8* | | *210/28* | |

**Bowling Record:**

| O | M | Runs | W | Avge |
|---|---|------|---|------|
| 3 | 1 | 16 | 0 | -- |

| 5wI | 10wM |
|-----|------|
| - | - |

**Career Best Performances:**
185 v. Cambridge University, Hove, 1996
*89\* v. Leicestershire, Hove, 1995 (SL)*
Best season 1990: 63 dismissals (ct 53 st 10)

Peter Moores was educated at King Edward VI School, Macclesfield and, after a short spell on the MCC groundstaff, he began his first-class cricket career with Worcestershire in 1983. When Steven Rhodes came to New Road in 1985, Peter realised that his first-team chances would be limited and he left to join Sussex. Ian Gould was then 'keeping for Sussex, but Peter played well for the Second XI and in 1987 he was given a run in the County side. He started to do well there and in 1989 he scored his first hundred, 116 against Somerset at Hove, and dismissed 58 batsmen.

The 1990 season saw him established as the County's First XI keeper, the scorer of nearly 700 runs and he had 63 dismissals to his credit. Throughout the 1990s he was an established wicketkeeper/batsman and was mentioned in the media as a possible Test player, although the closest he came to representative cricket was in fact with an MCC tour to Namibia, the Leeward Islands and Bahrain. In 1994, in the Championship match with Gloucestershire at Bristol, he equalled his own record against Yorkshire at Middlesbrough in 1991 by taking eight catches in the match and he went into the Sussex record books alongside Harry Butt, Rupert Webb and Arnold Long.

The Sussex AGM in the spring of 1997 was a torrid occasion which led to the removal of the committee and the loss of Alan Wells and other important players from Sussex's ranks. At the beginning of the new season, Peter found himself captaining an under-strength and somewhat demoralised side. Despite the fact that the County finished bottom of both the County Championship and the Sunday League, there were many who felt that Peter had not only made the best of a bad job, but had held things together sufficiently well that there was some real hope for the future. Many more thought he deserved a medal for it.

In the following season, Chris Adams came from Derbyshire to take over the captaincy from Peter, and after a few games he handed over the gloves to his protégé Shaun Humphries, and became County coach, a post that he continues to hold. His ability in this area was recognised by his invitation to act as coach to the England 'A' team in the West Indies in the winter of 2000/2001.

# William L. Murdoch
### RHB, RM & WK, 1893-99

**Born:** Sandhurst, Victoria, Australia, 18 October 1854
**Died:** Yarra Park, Melbourne, Australia, 18 February 1911

**County Captain:** 1893-1899
**Batting Record:**

| M | I | NO | Runs | Avge |
|---|---|----|------|------|
| 137 | 249 | 14 | 5,799 | 24.67 |

| 100 | 50 | | CT/ST | |
|-----|----|--|-------|--|
| 5 | 32 | | 51 | |

**Bowling Record:**

| O | M | Runs | W | Avge |
|---|---|------|---|------|
| 26 | 7 | 85 | 1 | 85.00 |

**Career Best Performances:**
226 v. Cambridge University, Hove, 1895
8-2-26-1 v. Somerset, Hove, 1896 (5 balls to the over)

William Murdoch, 'Billy' to his friends like Dr W.G. Grace, was a great character who, it was said, could bring genuine and unaffected humour to any dressing-room. He was also the first Australian to rank with England's best batsmen. He first played for Australia in 1877 and became captain in 1880. He led his country on sixteen occasions and made five tours of England. A right-handed batsman, he was a stylist who possessed a good eye and superb footwork and scored 321 for New South Wales against Victoria in 1881/82, the highest score recorded in Australian cricket until twenty years later. Not content with that record, he made the first double hundred in Test cricket when he scored 211 against England at the Oval in 1884, having two years previously made 286 not out for the Australians against Sussex. After the 1884 season, and following his marriage, little was seen of him in first-class cricket until he returned to lead Australia in the 1890 tour of England. Soon afterwards he decided to settle in England, changed his allegiance and toured South Africa with W.W. Read's team in 1891/92, playing for England in the only Test of that tour.

In 1893, he assumed the Sussex captaincy and played for seven seasons, passing 1,000 runs in two of them. Of his five centuries for the County, his 226 against Cambridge University in 1895, where *Wisden* referred to his 'playing a great game and showing his beautifully stylish and correct batting', was undoubtedly the best, and during this innings he shared in three separate partnerships of over one hundred runs. His captaincy was top-class too, and the continued improvement in the form of Walter Humphreys, the lob-bowler, may well have been aided by Billy's thoughtful approach.

In 1899, his form deserted him and, after only seven county games, he handed over the captaincy to Ranji. He was a lawyer by profession, and after 1899 he gave up county cricket and appeared for W.G. Grace's London County Club from 1901 to 1904. Such was his fine physique that one might have thought he would live to a greater age than fifty-six, but having returned to Australia, he was a spectator at a Test match against South Africa at Melbourne in February 1911, and during the luncheon interval he collapsed and died soon afterwards. But he did not remain in Australia: his remains were embalmed and brought to England to be buried at Kensal Green in London.

# William (Billy) Newham
*RHB & RM, 1881-1905*

**Born:** Shrewsbury, Shropshire, 12 December 1860
**Died:** Portslade, 26 June 1944

**County Captain:** 1889 and 1891-92

**Batting Record:**

| M | I | NO | Runs | Avge |
|---|---|----|------|------|
| 334 | 583 | 39 | 13,739 | 25.25 |
| 100 | 50 | | CT/ST | |
| 18 | 70 | | 159 | |

**Bowling Record:**

| O | M | Runs | W | Avge |
|---|---|------|---|------|
| 274 | 93 | 615 | 10 | 61.50 |

**Career Best Performances:**
201* v. Somerset, Hove, 1896
35-18-57-3 v. Surrey, The Oval, 1885 (4 balls to the over)

Billy Newham's service to Sussex cricket is almost certainly unsurpassed. From the time of his debut for the County in 1881 until his death in 1944, when he was still acting as assistant secretary, he had been a loyal servant for sixty-three years. Billy was born in Shropshire, but began his connection with Sussex as a pupil at Ardingly College and he did not leave there (by which time he was a master) until 1887. He made his debut for the County in 1881 and was the mainstay of the batting throughout the 1880s. Of medium height and well built, he displayed exceptional skill against fast bowling, driving hard on both sides of the wicket, cutting brilliantly and, when playing back, forcing the ball past mid-on or off his legs. He led the Sussex averages on three occasions in the 1880s and, by the time Fry and Ranji were playing in the last decade of the nineteenth century, he was part of a very powerful batting unit, particularly when playing at home on the batsman-friendly Hove wicket. In 1896, he scored 201 not out against Somerset at Hove, and in that and in the following year he passed 1,000 runs for the season.

Strangely, however, two of his lasting achievements were made away from Hove. In 1894, batting against Lancashire at Old Trafford, he took out his bat for 110 from a total of 174, his innings at the time being described as a remarkable combination of resolute hitting and skilful defence against deadly bowling by Mold and Briggs; then in 1902, when he was 41, he scored 153 in a partnership of 344 with Ranji (230) against Essex at Leyton, a record that is still the highest seventh-wicket stand in England. An outstanding fielder in the deep, Billy's athleticism was also demonstrated on the soccer field, where he represented Sussex and the Corinthians at full back.

In 1889 Billy became Sussex's captain/secretary and, although he was pleased to hand over the captaincy to Billy Murdoch in 1893, he remained as secretary until 1908. After that he became assistant secretary and was still doing work of this sort at the time of his death in 1944.

He did not figure greatly in representative cricket. He played for the Gentlemen at Lord's, the Oval and Hastings and in 1886/87 he toured Australia under Arthur Shrewsbury, appearing in his sole Test at Sydney. But his abiding achievement is the service he rendered to Sussex over such a long period.

# Charles Oakes
## *RHB & LBG, 1935-54*

**Born:** Horsham, 10 August 1912

**County Cap:** 1937

**Batting Record:**

| M | I | NO | Runs | Avge |
|---|---|---|---|---|
| 285 | 468 | 40 | 10,728 | 25.06 |
| 100 | 50 | | CT/ST | |
| 14 | 44 | | 159 | |

**Bowling Record:**

| O | M | Runs | W | Avge |
|---|---|---|---|---|
| 4,338 | 714 | 14,119 | 449 | 31.44 |
| 5wI | 10wM | | | |
| 16 | - | | | |

**Career Best Performances:**
160 v. Glamorgan, Chichester, 1950
21.3-1-147-8 v. Kent, Tonbridge, 1939

Charles Oakes, the eldest son of Alfred 'Joker' Oakes, for many years the Horsham groundsman, was brought up with three brothers and one sister in the white-painted cottage at the edge of the ground. He joined the County in 1935, but did not make a breakthrough until 1937, when he scored over 600 runs, a first Championship hundred and took 37 wickets. The next two pre-war years showed similar progress, although he often conceded too many runs even though he was taking wickets. He took 8 wickets against Kent in 1939, but went for nearly 7 runs an over.

His career was interrupted at a vital stage by the Second World War. Aged twenty-seven at the start, he was not back on a cricket field, having served in the RAF, until he was almost thirty-four. Yet he had matured, and retirements, especially that of Jim Parks senior, meant that the number three slot was his for the taking and his spin bowling formed a vital element in the County's attack. He was often styled as a hard-hitting right hand batsman (which was correct) and a leg-break and googly bowler (which was largely incorrect). Charles' leg-breaks, which batsmen could hear humming through the air, were mainly top-spinners and googlies. Like some leggies before him, he rather lost the basic delivery in favour of the more esoteric spin.

From 1946 to 1950, he scored over 1,000 runs every season – 1,543 in 1950 was his best return – and he was usually well among the wickets; 1950 was also his best season with the ball when he took 72 wickets. In 1948, the press spoke about his probable selection for the MCC South Africa tour in the following winter, but it came to nothing and he had to content himself with county cricket. Not that he shirked it; he rarely missed a game for Sussex and often played for other teams at each end of the season. Those who knew him well saw him as a charming, laid-back man who often dropped off to sleep while waiting his turn to bat and was sometimes woken up by mischievous cries from the younger players of 'Charlie, you're in now', when in fact he wasn't!

After 1950, his performances eased down somewhat and at the end of the 1954 season he retired and for a spell followed his father as Horsham groundsman before finally finding a niche as a respected coach at Stowe School.

# Alan S.M. Oakman

*RHB & OB, 1947-68*

**Born:** Hastings, 20 April 1930

**County Cap:** 1951

**Batting Record:**

| M | I | NO | Runs | W |
|---|---|---|---|---|
| 497 | 847 | 76 | 20,117 | 26.09 |
| *16* | *16* | *2* | *318* | *22.71* |
| **100** | **50** | | **CT/ST** | |
| 20 | 44 | | 562 | |
| - | *2* | | *6* | |

**Bowling Record:**

| O | M | Runs | W | Avge |
|---|---|---|---|---|
| 7,746 | 2,324 | 19,200 | 703 | 27.31 |
| *20* | *5* | *54* | *3* | *18.00* |
| **5wI** | **10wM** | | | |
| 31 | 2 | | | |
| - | - | | | |

**Career Best Performances:**
229* v. Nottinghamshire, Worksop, 1961
*57 v. Middlesex, Hove, 1967 (GC)*
27-12-39-7 v. Glamorgan, Eastbourne, 1954
*6-1-28-2 v. Durham, Hove, 1964 (GC)*

Alan Oakman first played for Sussex as a seventeen-year-old in 1947, but it was not until 1950, after National Service with the Guards, that he started to command a regular place. In 1951 and 1952, he took over 75 wickets for Sussex each year and did the hat-trick against Somerset. In 1952 he also missed his maiden century by just one run. During 1953 he appeared to be on course for 100 wickets in the season, but a broken thumb kept him out of the game after late July. Then in 1954, Robin Marlar, also an off-break bowler, appeared for Sussex and it looked as though Alan would bowl rather less than he had done previously. However, a fine run in the latter part of the season, including his career best of 7 for 39 against Glamorgan, meant that he wound up with 95 wickets. He did, however, start to bowl less as Marlar showed his mettle in the following seasons; fortunately, as Alan's bowling declined, so his batting started to prosper.

He reached his first hundred in 1955 and in the next season he scored five centuries, including 178 against Glamorgan, together with 80 for MCC against the Australians. This led to his inclusion in England's Test team, batting at number three in his first match, bowling a little – spin bowling was largely in the capable hands of the Surrey spin-twins – and

fielding close with tremendous success. He was, of course, involved in 'Laker's Match' at Old Trafford in which he took five catches at short-leg. In the following winter he was included in the MCC side to South Africa, but injury led to his not doing himself justice. From then on it was county cricket and nothing more.

In the late 1950s and early 1960s, Alan's bowling was little in evidence, but his batting and his fielding came on well and he took over 50 catches in each of the 1958 and 1959 seasons. His first double hundred, 229 not out against Nottinghamshire, came in 1961 and he reached over 2,000 runs for the season. With Marlar's virtual retirement in 1961, Alan returned to off-spinning. He took 55 wickets in 1963 and continued to do his share until close upon his retirement in 1968. With the advent of limited-overs cricket, he was very much part of Sussex's success in the early years of the Gillette Cup, and sometimes opened the batting. After his retirement he became a first-class umpire and a respected coach with Warwickshire.

# Paul W.G. Parker
### RHB & RM/LB, 1976-91

**Born:** Bulawayo, Zimbabwe, 15 January 1956

**County Cap:** 1979
**County Captain:** 1988-1991

**Batting Record:**

| M | I | NO | Runs | Avge |
|---|---|---|---|---|
| 289 | 494 | 67 | 15,150 | 35.48 |
| 284 | 272 | 34 | 7,332 | 30.81 |
| **100** | **50** | | **CT/ST** | |
| 37 | 69 | | 204 | |
| 6 | 49 | | 102 | |

**Bowling Record:**

| O | M | Runs | W | Avge |
|---|---|---|---|---|
| 80 | 13 | 364 | 5 | 72.80 |
| 8.5 | 0 | 61 | 5 | 12.20 |

**Career Best Performances:**
181 v. Sri Lankans, Hove, 1984
*121\* v. Northamptonshire, Hastings, 1983 (SL)*
7-2-21-2 v. Surrey, Guildford, 1984
*1-0-3-2 v. Minor Counties, Hove, 1987 (B &H)*

In 1981, Paul Parker played for England in the Sixth Test against Australia at the Oval. As was to befall his County colleague, Alan Wells, fourteen years later, one Test was considered by England's selectors to be a fair assessment of a player's ability at the highest level.

Paul's record for Sussex was rather different. Educated at Collyer's School, Horsham, he moved on to Cambridge University, for whom he scored 215 (his maiden century) against Essex and 148 off a strong Yorkshire attack in 1976. He would also have won a blue at rugby but for injury. A new star seemed to be on the horizon. While at Cambridge he began playing for the County and from 1979 until 1991, when he left, he was a permanent fixture in the side, scoring over 1,000 runs in six seasons with 1,692 in 1984 his best return. To these figures must be added the innumerable runs he saved in the field, as for much of this period he was the outstanding cover fielder in the country.

In 1988 he took over the captaincy, which seemed a logical appointment for a man of his experience. Sadly, the County's results during his tenure were largely below par, being no better than 11th place in the 1991 Championship and in the 1989 Sunday League. Unsurprisingly, therefore, at the end of the 1991 season, he was replaced as captain by Alan Wells. Ingenuously, perhaps, the committee thought he would like to remain as a player, but Paul, in common with the majority of deposed captains, did not agree and he joined the fledgling county of Durham in 1992, where he played with distinction for two seasons before returning to the south to teach Classics at Tonbridge School.

He achieved much in first-class cricket and just as much in the limited-overs game, not least possessing a fine big match temperament for one-day finals. When Sussex reached Lord's in 1978, they were facing a Somerset side with Richards, Botham and Garner, but the Sussex bowlers kept them down to 207 for 7 wickets. After an excellent opening partnership, it was Paul's 62 not out that carried the County to victory by 5 wickets in the 54th over. Eight years later, in the NatWest Trophy final, Lancashire posted an imposing 242, but the County were up to the challenge and Paul's 85 had, according to *Wisden*, 'the sonority of a strokemaker in form' and played an essential part in the 7-wicket victory.

# Henry W. (Harry) Parks

*RHB & RM, 1926-48*

HARRY PARKS

**Born:** Haywards Heath, 18 July 1906
**Died:** Taunton, Somerset, 7 May 1984

**Batting Record:**

| M | I | NO | Runs | Avge |
|---|---|----|------|------|
| 480 | 740 | 97 | 21,692 | 33.74 |
| **100** | **50** | | **CT/ST** | |
| 42 | 106 | | 195 | |

**Bowling Record:**

| O | M | Runs | W | Avge |
|---|---|------|---|------|
| 213 | 34 | 705 | 13 | 54.23 |
| **5wI** | **10wM** | | | |
| - | - | | | |

**Career Best Performances:**
200* v. Essex, Chelmsford, 1931
9-0-37-2 v. Cambridge University, Cambridge, 1928

Harry Parks, the younger brother of Jim senior, was an important member of this notable Sussex cricketing family. From 1926 to 1948 he was a consistent middle-order batsman and a brilliant outfield. He made his first century and scored a 1,000 runs in 1928 and although he lost his place in 1929, he came back strongly in 1930 and scored 1,000 runs in every season until his retirement. He still appears in two record stands for the County: in 1930, Harry (71) and Bert Wensley (120) put on 178 for the 9th wicket against Derbyshire and in 1937 he joined his brother Jim (168) in a 5th wicket stand of 297 against Hampshire, his own share being 155. Other large stands included 239 in 1931 with Duleepsinhji (140) against Essex, his own score being 200 not out; and 307 in 1939, when Harry (127) partnered John Langridge (160) against Kent. However, arguably his best performance in the pre-war period was the match with Essex at Leyton in 1933. Facing the host's total of 560 for 9 wickets declared, Sussex had replied with 402 and were invited to follow on. Batting again,

Sussex eventually declared at 285 for 6 wickets and drew the match. Harry had made 114 not out in the first innings and 105 not out in the second. Scoring two unbeaten hundreds in a match was something which only four other batsmen had then achieved.

In 1939, Harry joined the RAF and reached the rank of Flight Lieutenant. Returning to Sussex in 1946, he opened with John Langridge for three seasons and, in 1947, now aged forty-one, he reached 2,000 runs in all matches for the first time. After making an excellent 61 against the powerful 1948 Australians, he decided to retire at the end of the season. For two years he was a first-class umpire and from 1951 to 1954 head coach with Somerset. Following a short period with Devonshire, he became coach at Taunton School until he retired for good.

In Harry's obituary in *Wisden*, the writer opines that he illustrated what one meant by 'a good *county* player' and that, in 1985 (when the text was written) few spectators would have any vivid memory of any innings they saw him play. Those who saw him bat against Worcestershire at Horsham in 1947, belabouring the floated leg-breaks of Roly Jenkins and hitting 3 sixes and 16 fours in a magnificent innings of 170, might take a different view.

**Born:** Haywards Heath, 12 May 1903
**Died:** Cuckfield, 21 November 1980

**Batting Record:**

| M | I | NO | Runs | Avge |
|---|---|---|---|---|
| 434 | 702 | 60 | 19,720 | 30.77 |
| **100** | **50** | | **CT/ST** | |
| 39 | 80 | | 302 | |

**Bowling Record:**

| O | M | Runs | W | Avge |
|---|---|---|---|---|
| 9,200 | 2,660 | 21,292 | 795 | 26.78 |
| **5wI** | **10wM** | | | |
| 23 | 1 | | | |

**Career Best Performances:**
197 v. Kent, Hastings, 1936
24-15-17-7 v. Leicestershire, Horsham, 1924

James Parks senior will always be remembered for one unique achievement. In the 1937 season, he scored 3,003 runs (average 50.89), including 11 centuries, and took 101 wickets at 25.83 each. Unless the format of the County Championship changes radically, it is unlikely that his record will ever be equalled. His son, 'Young Jim' recalls that his father's remarkable season may have been a reaction to a family bereavement. 'Mother had died in the previous year and Dad just threw himself into his cricket to try and forget the loss.' In his record-breaking season, he was called up to play for England in the First Test at Lord's against New Zealand. He opened the batting with Len Hutton (also making his debut), scored 27 and 7, took three wickets for 36 runs off 21 overs and was promptly dropped. It was hardly a test of his ability.

Jim was in his late teens when he started to think seriously about a career in cricket and a good performance against Sussex's Club and Ground XI in his home town of Haywards Heath attracted the interest of the County. He made his debut in 1924 and in only his third match he took 7 Leicestershire wickets for 17 runs off 24 overs at Horsham. But it was then slow going and not until 1927 did he first make 1,000 runs and take over 40 wickets with his slow medium off-cutters and in-swingers. From then until 1939 he was an indispensable member of the County side. He often opened the batting: in 1929 he made 110 in a partnership with Ted Bowley (280) in just over three hours against Gloucestershire and, later on, he formed a regular partnership with John Langridge and also became known as an excellent close fielder.

In 1935 he did the double and represented the Players at Lord's, and in 1935/36 he was a member of E.R.T. Holmes' MCC side that toured Australasia; he played in the four unofficial Tests against New Zealand. His first-class career ended in 1939. Jim was posted to Accrington during the war; when he was not re-engaged by Sussex in 1946, he stayed in Lancashire and played league cricket there, before becoming Nottinghamshire's coach and then spending three years as a first-class umpire. After an absence of twenty-four years he returned to Sussex as coach and was reunited with his son, Jim, who was by then an established member of the County team.

# James Michael (Young Jim) Parks
*RHB, LB & WK, 1949-72*

**Born:** Haywards Heath, 21 October 1931

**County Cap:** 1951
**County Captain:** 1967-68

**Batting Record:**

| M | I | NO | Runs | Avge |
|---|---|----|------|------|
| 563 | 948 | 138 | 29,138 | 35.97 |
| *89* | *84* | *7* | *1,982* | *25.74* |
| **100** | **50** | | **CT/ST** | |
| 42 | 175 | | 872/65 | |
| *1* | *11* | | *89/3* | |

**Bowling Record:**

| O | M | Runs | W | Avge |
|---|---|------|---|------|
| 518 | 109 | 1700 | 42 | 40.47 |
| **5wI** | **10wM** | | | |
| - | - | | | |

**Career Best Performances:**
205* v. Somerset, Hove, 1955
*102* v. Durham, Hove, 1964*
16.5-6-23-3 v. Cambridge University, Hove, 1956
Best Season 1959: 93 dismissals (ct 86, st 7)

James Michael Parks was the most successful of a loyal sporting family whose playing connection with the County lasted from 1924 to 1972 and amounted to more than 70,000 runs. A prodigy at Hove County School, Jim once made 82 not out and took 8 wickets for 2 runs in a house match; consequently, it was no surprise that Sussex snapped him up when he was only seventeen. His father, 'Old Jim', was, however, absolutely determined that his son did not blindly follow the family tradition into cricket. 'Dad was anxious that I was sincere in my ambition to be a county cricketer.'

Jim first played for Sussex in 1949, and in the following season he made a sparkling 159 not out against Kent. In 1951, still only nineteen, he joined his skipper, Jim Langridge, in a partnership of 294 against Kent at Tunbridge Wells. His own innings of 188 led directly to the award of his county cap. In this period he was also gaining wider experience during National Service of playing for the RAF and Combined Services, rubbing shoulders with players such as Ray Illingworth and Fred Trueman. In 1953, now playing full-time for Sussex, he reached his first 1,000 runs for the season. His sparkling stroke play, which included a marvellous cover-drive despite his front-on stance, soon attracted the attention of the England selectors and he played his first Test against Pakistan in 1954.

In the next two seasons, despite an 'A' team tour, he missed out on Test cricket, but scored heavily elsewhere, completing over 2,000 runs in 1955 and excelling with an innings of 205 not out against Somerset at Hove, hitting 5 sixes and 25 fours in a glorious display of stroke-play. He was selected to tour South Africa with Peter May's MCC team in the winter of 1956/57, but this marked a low point in his career and led, quite unfairly, to accusations of 'cold feet'. The facts were different: before the tour began he had suffered a blow to the head playing football and at the start of the tour in Cape Town a spectator deflected a ball onto his head during fielding practice. This led to double-vision and he was sent back to England. When it was time to return to South Africa, he was suffering from influenza and he collapsed in the aircraft at London Airport. Described by the press as faint-hearted, he was taken to hospital where he was found to be suffering from pneumonia. Suddenly his tour ended. And so, for the moment, did his

*Jim Parks* (left) *shows the power of his square-drive and* (right) *behind the stumps, where he served both Sussex and England with distinction.*

potentially promising Test career.

In the following few seasons, Jim continued to lead the Sussex batting, twice making 2,000 runs in a season and often figuring among the top batsmen of the national averages. In 1958, Sussex's regular wicketkeeper was injured and he took over the gloves in an emergency. He proved so successful that, at the age of twenty-eight, another dimension to his career appeared. He had hoped to be included in the MCC team, again led by Peter May, to tour the West Indies in 1959/60 but, when not chosen, he accepted instead a coaching post with the Trinidad Cricket Council. This time fate was not against him. The MCC manager asked him to fly to Georgetown to cover for Ken Barrington who was unwell prior to the Fourth Test. Ken, in fact, did play, but Jim scored 183 in the next MCC match against Berbice and, when the party moved back to Trinidad, he found himself included as wicketkeeper for the final Test. Scoring 101 not out in England's second innings, he found that he had virtually cemented himself in England's Test team. From 1960 through until 1967/68 in the West Indies,

when he finally surrendered his Test spot to Alan Knott, he played a further 44 Test matches, although three other 'keepers, especially John Murray, played at times for England.

Jim never let his involvement with England dim his efforts for Sussex. His style made him an ideal one-day batsman and, together with Ted Dexter, he formed a fearsome batting duo in the early days of the Gillette Cup, which Sussex won in the two inaugural years. In 1967, he was appointed captain of the County, but half way through the next season he found that dressing-room squabbles were a strain and affecting his form. He resigned his post and, at the end of the 1972 season, as a result of a disagreement over wicketkeeping, he left the county of his birth and joined Somerset. It was a sad moment, but he later accepted Sussex life membership and became the Club's marketing manager in the 1990s. Jim's record is quite remarkable: he scored 36,673 runs (average 34.76 and including 51 hundreds) in his career for Sussex, Somerset and England – a figure than has not been surpassed by any player who has played most of his cricket for the southern county.

# Nawab of Pataudi (Mansur Ali Khan)
*RHB & RM, 1957-70*

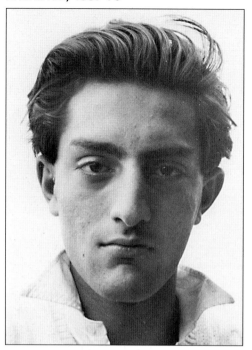

**Born:** Bhopal, India, 5 January 1941

**County Cap:** 1963
**County Captain:** 1966

**Batting Record:**

| M | I | NO | Runs | Avge |
|---|---|---|---|---|
| 88 | 150 | 13 | 3,054 | 22.29 |
| *5* | *4* | *0* | *114* | *28.50* |
| **100** | **50** | | **CT/ST** | |
| 1 | 14 | | 68 | |
| - | - | | *4* | |

**Bowling Record:**

| O | M | Runs | W | Avge |
|---|---|---|---|---|
| 10 | 2 | 43 | 0 | - |
| **5wI** | **10wM** | | | |
| - | - | | | |

**Career Best Performances:**
101 v. Hampshire, Portsmouth 1965
*42 v. Somerset, Taunton, 1966 and 42
v. Surrey, The Oval, 1970 (both GC)*

Mansur Ali Khan was the son of Iftiqar Ali Khan, who had played for England before captaining India in 1946. Mansur was educated at Winchester, coached there by George Cox, and in 1957 he played for Sussex at the age of 16 years 8 months. Only J.M. Mare in 1870 had been younger. He still had two full seasons at school after his first-class debut.

After Winchester, 'Tiger', as he became known, went up to Oxford and made a hundred when he won his first blue. He captained the University for two successive seasons – an unusual honour – and played for Sussex in the vacations.

In 1961, a car accident resulted, sadly, in the impairment of the sight in his right eye. With remarkable courage and common sense, he remodelled his stance so that his left shoulder pointed more towards mid-wicket, but this did not inhibit his off-side play. In fact, as early as 1961/62 he made his debut for India in the Third Test against England. By the Fifth Test he had made his first hundred and went on tour to the West Indies in the New Year. He took over the captaincy at the age of twenty-one and led his country against England two winters later, when he scored 203

not out in the Fourth Test. He continued to lead India with success against Australia and New Zealand.

He played little for Sussex in the early sixties, although he did win his cap in 1963, but in 1965 he was back, scoring over 1,000 runs and his first hundred for the County. When Ted Dexter resigned the captaincy at the end of 1965, he took over for 1966. It was perhaps a strange decision, but the committee was doubtless influenced by his excellent captaincy of India, and Sussex moved from 16th to 10th place in the Championship under his leadership. At the end of the season he handed over to Jim Parks as he was due to captain the Indians in England in 1967.

His appearances for Sussex became far less frequent. He continued to lead India throughout the 1960s and he played for them, occasionally as captain, until as late as 1975 This elegant and resourceful batsman was always something of a 'dasher', giving the fast bowlers a chance early in his innings, and his fielding was always magnificent. It must be said, however, that his contribution to Indian cricket was far greater than that which he made to Sussex.

# Henry (Harry) Phillips
*RHB, SLA & WK, 1868-91*

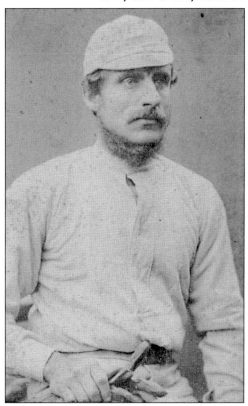

**Born:** Hastings, 14 October 1844
**Died:** Clive Vale, Hastings, 3 July 1919

**Batting Record:**

| M | I | NO | Runs | Avge |
|---|---|----|------|------|
| 195 | 335 | 69 | 2,895 | 10.88 |

| 100 | 50 | | CT/ST | |
|-----|----|--|-------|--|
| 1 | 5 | | 311/182 | |

**Bowling Record:**

| Runs | W | Avge |
|------|---|------|
| 283 | 14 | 20.21 |

**Career Best Performances:**
111 v. Australians, Hove, 1884
4-33 v. Surrey, Hove, 1868

There have been a good many 'firsts' in the game of cricket and Henry Phillips, Harry to the cricketing fraternity, was the originator of one – he was the first wicket-keeper to dispense with a long-stop. 'Phillips kept wicket so good that he used no longstop', a contemporary report noted after the match with Gloucestershire in 1873. One must perhaps assume that the 'keepers of the nineteenth century did not quite cut the athletic figure of men like Gilchrist and Boucher nowadays, but Harry, at only 5ft 4in and less than ten stone, was regarded in his day as nimble and astute, and was aided by the fact that he was ambidextrous and had particularly long arms. He was not, however, quite in the class of men like Pooley and Sherwin and representative cricket seldom came his way – two matches for the Players and a benefit match for John Lillywhite in 1871 were his sole appearances.

A cabinet-maker and upholsterer by trade, he lived in Hastings all his life and first assisted Sussex in 1868, continuing for them behind the stumps until 1888 and then occasionally until 1891. In 1871, he caught 13 and stumped 11 batsmen in five matches and, one year later, caught 5 and stumped 5 in the match with Surrey at the Oval. Twelve years later he caught 3 Kent batsmen and stumped 5 in the county match at Hove.

Harry, had he not been a 'keeper, might have done quite well as a bowler, his slow left-hand round-arm deliveries being noted as 'useful', and even 'extraordinary' in contemporary reports. His batting ability, however, was generally regarded as moderate, but he enjoyed one day of greatness. Batting at number nine, he scored 111 in the County's match with the Australians in July 1884, which secured him a gratuity of 21 guineas. He partnered the amateur G.N. Wyatt (112) in a stand which added 182 for 8th wicket from a total of 396, the highest score of the summer against the visitors. If this was the high spot of his batting, the match against Nottinghamshire in 1873, when the County were dismissed for 19, does him less credit as the scorecard read: 'H. Phillips ... absent, missed train 0'!

In June 1886, he was awarded a benefit in a 'Grand Match' against Gloucestershire (admission 6d), an event which netted him over £350 (including £100 from Lord Sheffield, the Club president), a not inconsiderable sum at the time.

# Anthony C.S. (Tony) Pigott

*RHB & RFM, 1978-93*

**Born:** Fulham, London, 4 June 1958

**County Cap:** 1982
**County Chief Executive:** 1997-1999

**Batting Record:**

| M | I | NO | Runs | Avge |
|---|---|----|------|------|
| 232 | 279 | 64 | 4,411 | 20.51 |
| *224* | *137* | *45* | *1,480* | *16.09* |
| 100 | 50 | | CT/ST | |
| 1 | 20 | | 115 | |
| - | 2 | | 72 | |

**Bowling Record:**

| O | M | Runs | W | Avge |
|---|---|------|---|------|
| 5,500 | 980 | 18,341 | 574 | 31.95 |
| *1,667.3* | *95* | *7,661* | *314* | *24.40* |
| 5wI | 10wM | | | |
| 21 | - | | | |
| *3* | *-* | | | |

**Career Best Performances:**
104* v. Warwickshire, Edgbaston, 1986
*53 v. Derbyshire, Hove, 1988 (NWT)*
20.1-4-74-7 v. Northamptonshire, Eastbourne, 1982
*7.4-0-24-5 v. Lancashire, Old Trafford, 1986 (SL)*

Many county cricketers find themselves 'released' when they have lost form, but few county cricketers land up playing in an overseas Test when not actually in the touring party; fewer return from their dismissal to become chief executive and even fewer do not last the course once they reach the top job. But that is, broadly, what happened to Tony Pigott at Sussex.

Educated at Harrow, he made his debut in 1978 at the age of nineteen against Somerset when he did not even get on to bowl, played one further match and arrived wicket-less at the Surrey match in late July. Achieving the hat-trick with his first three wickets in county cricket, he enlivened a lifeless match that Sussex only just failed to win.

In 1980, he suffered severe back pain and a top surgeon told him his cricketing days were over. He refused to accept the diagnosis, regained his fitness for 1982, took 61 wickets and was awarded his county cap. He did even better in 1983 with 72 wickets and over 400 runs, and in 1983/84 played in New Zealand. Suddenly summoned to Christchurch to play in the Second Test, as Graham Dilley was unfit, he snaffled two wickets, but he and his bride had to postpone their wedding, which had been due to take place on the Monday of the match.

His back injury then cost him two more seasons, but the period from 1986 until 1990 was probably the best of his career. A hundred in 1986, at least 450 runs each season and 50 wickets in three of the years – 74 in 1988 his best – indicated his progress. In limited-overs matches, he always bowled effectively and, when the occasion demanded, came up with quick runs as well. In the early 1990s, his form tailed off and, when he went for nearly 7 runs an over in the 1993 NatWest final, he received his cards, but joined Surrey for 1994.

The Sussex revolution in 1997, however, saw him suddenly back at Hove as chief executive, making all sorts of changes and demanding that players 'run through brick walls for Sussex.' He later brought the Australian Test cricketer, David Gilbert, to join him and what happened is not clear, but at the end of 1999 he vanished from the scene almost as quickly as he had arrived, leaving David to lead Sussex into calmer waters.

# Kumar Shri (Ranji) Ranjitsinhji
## RHB & SRA, 1895-1920

**Born:** Sarodar, India, 10 September 1872
**Died:** Jamnagar, India, 2 April 1933

**County Captain:** 1899-1903

**Batting Record:**

| M | I | NO | Runs | Avge |
|---|---|----|------|------|
| 211 | 337 | 43 | 18,594 | 63.24 |

| 100 | 50 | | CT/ST | |
|-----|----|--|-------|--|
| 58 | 77 | | 157 | |

**Bowling Record:**

| O | M | Runs | W | Avge |
|---|---|------|---|------|
| 1,267 | 316 | 3,848 | 112 | 34.35 |

| 5wI | 10wM |
|-----|------|
| 3 | - |

**Career Best Performances:**
285* v. Somerset, Taunton 1901
32-8-109-6 v. MCC, Lord's 1895

Many have assumed that K.S. Ranjitsinhji, 'Ranji' in the world of cricket, came from princely stock in India and appeared as such in the 1890s on the English cricketing scene. This is not exactly the case. He was born in relatively lowly circumstances in Sarodar, a remote village in Western India, but as a small boy he went to live with his uncle. At the age of six he enjoyed a stroke of good fortune. He was selected as a temporary heir to a distant relative, the Jam Sahib of Nawanagar, as a precaution against the ruler failing to have any offspring of his own. When Ranji was ten, however, a son was born to the Jam Sahib and the opportunity seemed to have been lost, but in 1906 the son, the new Jam Sahib, died without an heir and, after some legal wrangling, Ranji succeeded to the title.

His second stroke of good fortune was that his uncle secured a place for him at Rajkumar College, a school for Indian princes that was run like an English public school. The headmaster recognised Ranji's talents and in 1888 he arranged for him to continue his education at a Cambridge school, from where he moved on to Trinity College. His cricket did not immediately come to the fore. In fact, he played for local sides before he gained a place in the University XI and did not win his blue until 1893. Two years

later, Ranji joined Sussex. On his debut for the County he scored 77 and 150 against MCC and he became a regular member of the team. Although initially a somewhat unorthodox batsman, he was blessed with exceptionally keen eyesight and flexible and powerful wrists which allowed him to glance the good length ball off the middle stump in a manner that few others have equalled; he was also a magnificent cutter and driver of the ball.

His skill soon brought him selection for England. In the Second Test against Australia in 1896 he scored 62 and 154 not out, becoming only the second batsman, after Dr. W.G. Grace, to score a century on his England debut. In 1897/98 he toured Australia and top-scored in the First Test with an impressive 175, made in only three and a half hours. From then until 1902, he was a fixture in the England side and in his 15 matches for his adopted country he scored 989 runs at an average of 44.95. It was, however, for Sussex that he made the bulk of his runs. He made 2,780 runs with 10 centuries in 1896, 3,159 with 8 centuries in 1899 (the first time that a batsman had exceeded 3,000 runs in a season), 3,065 with 11 centuries in 1900 and 2,077 with 8 centuries in 1904. He passed

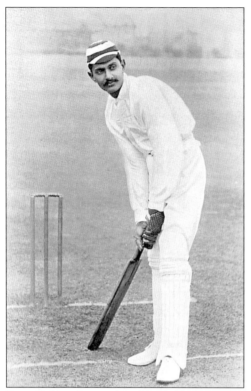 

*Ranji (left) in his youth and (right), now aged nearly forty, cuts a broader figure as he goes out to bat for Sussex v. Surrey at the Oval in 1912.*

1,000 runs in twelve seasons and captained Sussex between 1899 and 1903. Unsurprisingly, he often topped the national averages and in his career for Sussex between 1895 and 1920 he scored 18,594 runs (average 63.24) with 58 centuries and a top score of 285 not out against Somerset. No other Sussex batsman who has played a significant number of innings has come near equalling his record.

In 1907, Ranji succeeded to the title of Jam Sahib of Nawanagar, the responsibilities of which claimed much of his time, but Ranji was emotionally more tied to England than to India and he returned to Sussex in 1908 and 1912 to resume playing cricket. In the First World War, he identified with the British cause and became ADC to Sir John French, the Commander of the BEF. On leave in this country he joined a hunting party and, sadly, lost the sight of one eye in an accident. Back in England in 1920, he played two games for Sussex, but the dark-skinned, panther-like and elegant batsman, now

nearly forty-eight and quite stockily-built, showed a mere trace of his former ability. He played his final innings at Hastings, where in 1906 he had scored 234 not out against Surrey and said: 'I think I could have stayed there for ever, for the ball looked as a big as a balloon the whole time I was in.' History did not repeat itself and, batting at number eight, he made just a single against Northamptonshire.

From then until his death in 1933, Ranji devoted himself to the affairs of Nawanagar and represented India at the League of Nations. His small state prospered during his stewardship, although some say that the credit for its success was largely due to the British administrator at his court. Perhaps the last word should go to Sidney Southerton, *Wisden's* editor in 1934, who wrote: 'To me, Ranjitsinhji was the embodiment of all that a cricketer should be – generous in defeat, modest in success and genuinely enthusiastic regarding the achievements of either colleagues or opponents.'

# Dermot A. Reeve
## RHB & RMF, 1983-87

**Born:** Kowloon, Hong Kong, 2 April 1963

**County Cap:** 1986

**Batting Record:**

| M | I | NO | Runs | Avge |
|---|---|----|------|------|
| 91 | 101 | 31 | 1,761 | 25.15 |
| *87* | *45* | *19* | *348* | *13.38* |

| 100 | 50 | | CT/ST |
|-----|----|--|-------|
| 1 | 11 | | 51 |
| - | - | | 22 |

**Bowling Record:**

| O | M | Runs | W | Avge |
|---|---|------|---|------|
| 2,496 | 647 | 6,728 | 239 | 28.15 |
| *644.3* | *52* | *2,799* | *101* | *27.71* |

| 5wI | 10wM |
|-----|------|
| 5 | 0 |
| - | - |

**Career Best Performances:**
119 v. Surrey, Guildford, 1984
*30* v. Kent, Canterbury, 1987 (B&H)*
21-6-37-7 v. Lancashire, Lytham, 1987
*12-4-20-4 v. Lancashire, Lord's, 1986 (NWT final)*

Dermot Reeve's enthusiasm and determination to succeed at the game of cricket, has been the keystone of his career. He tells a story about himself, that Imran Khan, with whom he played at Sussex, said after the 1992 World Cup Final: 'You have done really well for a player of such limited ability'. This put-down was not meant in any unkind manner, but there was probably more than a grain of truth in it.

Dermot, educated at the King George V School in Kowloon where he was captain of cricket, joined the Lord's groundstaff on arrival in England. Recommended by Ian Gould, who had faced his bowling in the nets, he joined Sussex in 1983 and took 42 and 55 wickets respectively in his first two seasons as well as scoring a maiden century, 119 against Surrey, after he had been sent in at number three as a nightwatchman. In general, however, his batting opportunities were restricted, especially in limited-overs matches, as he was often in the lower half of the order. After a steady season in 1985, he again reached 50 wickets in 1986 and

showed real form in the NatWest final at Lord's when his 4 for 20 earned him the man of the match award. With the first ball of his third over he trapped former Sussex batsman, Gehan Mendis, for 17 and with the fifth he dismissed the illustrious Clive Lloyd, also lbw and for a duck. *Wisden* commented that 'he bowled commendably to a full length on a slow pitch, obtaining movement both ways off the seam'.

Sadly, however, he was starting to become disillusioned. He complained that the Hove wicket gave little assistance to his bowling (had the sea fret perhaps never helped his swing?) and he refused to sign for 1988, preferring instead to join Warwickshire. It was a blow to the County, all the more savage because they had dispensed with the services of Ian Greig two years previously, in the belief that Dermot had the better long-term future.

At Edgbaston, however, Dermot enjoyed a spectacular career. He played there for nine seasons, improved his batting beyond all recognition, won three Test caps and played in 29 limited-overs internationals, and as captain from 1993 he won a stack of trophies for his new county. Ironically, it was his 81 not out which was largely instrumental in snatching the NatWest Trophy from Sussex off the very last ball in the 1993 final.

# Albert E. Relf

*RHB & RM, 1900-21*

**Born:** Brightling, 26 June 1874
**Died:** Wellington College, Berkshire, 26 March 1937

**Batting Record:**

| M | I | NO | Runs | Avge |
|---|---|----|------|------|
| 448 | 719 | 54 | 18,133 | 27.22 |
| **100** | **50** | | **CT/ST** | |
| 22 | 95 | | 409 | |

**Bowling Record:**

| O | M | Runs | W | Avge |
|---|---|------|---|------|
| 15,241 | 5,144 | 33,410 | 1,594 | 20.95 |
| **5wI** | **10wM** | | | |
| 99 | 20 | | | |

**Career Best Performances:**
189* v. Hampshire, Portsmouth, 1906
40-9-95-9 v. Warwickshire, Hove, 1910

Not quite the batsman that Joe Vine was in his time and marginally below Maurice Tate as a bowler a few years later, Albert Relf was nevertheless Sussex's leading all-rounder in the first twenty-one years of the twentieth century. When he began his career with the County in 1900, at the age of twenty-five, he was already a seasoned cricketer. Tutored by his father, the coach at Wellington College, he had tried his luck in Newmarket, in Ireland and finally in Kent before becoming an employee of the Earl of Wilton in Norfolk. Having previously received little encouragement from Sussex, he qualified for Norfolk in 1898. In the following year, having done so well in his adopted county, he caught the eye of the Lord's authorities and joined the groundstaff there before making his Championship debut for Sussex in 1900 and scoring 96 against Worcestershire.

He joined the side primarily as a batsman and, despite being criticised for his somewhat inelegant style, he made more runs season after season than many a player who looked vastly superior. Between 1902 and 1914, he exceeded 1,000 runs in a season on eight occasions and achieved the unusual record of participating in a century partnership for every wicket down the order. In the field he was an exceptional slip-fielder, but it was really as a bowler that he made his mark. He adapted so quickly to the county game that by 1903 he was heading the bowling averages with 108 wickets in all matches. He achieved 100 wickets on a further nine occasions, 146 in 1910 (average 19.71) being his best return. Now a formidable all-rounder, he achieved the double of 1,000 runs and 100 wickets in six seasons between 1905 and 1913. He bowled at medium-pace off a short run, moving the ball both ways, while maintaining a perfect control of line and length. On a crumbling wicket he was said to be almost unplayable and C.B. Fry noted that his pace was deceptive – faster than expected on a hard wicket, yet slower than the flight suggested on a heavy wicket. His easy delivery allowed him to bowl tirelessly for hours on end – in 1910, *Wisden* noted that 'Relf is a bowler who never tires of his task.'

His bowling feats were remarkable: 1902 – a hat-trick against Worcestershire; 1906 – an analysis of 54 overs 29 maidens and 4 for 49 against Yorkshire at Bradford; 1910 – 9 Warwickshire wickets for 95; 1912 – 15 wickets (8 for 41 and 7 for 36) against Leicestershire; 1920, then aged forty-six – 85.1 overs 38 maidens and 9 for 93 in seven hours of bowling in the two Essex innings. All of these perfor-

Left: *Albert Relf looks ready for a social occasion.* Right: *Relf* (right) *gives some advice to Jim Langridge at Hove in the 1930s.*

mances, except the one against Yorkshire, were on the Hove wicket, were generally regarded as a batsman's paradise.

After the First World War, having succeeded his father as coach at Wellington College, he was able to play only in the school holidays and he ended his career in 1921. His total of 1594 wickets places him third behind Maurice Tate and George Cox senior in the County's leading wicket-takers. He was a glutton for work: apart from his Test caps, he represented the Players, MCC and numerous other teams so that, for instance, in 1910 he played 56 first-class innings and bowled 1,250 overs, taking 158 wickets altogether. He was one of *Wisden's* Cricketers of the Year in 1913.

It was unfortunate that Albert's career coincided with that of Sydney Barnes. In 1903, C.B. Fry and Ranji recommended him for the MCC Australian tour of the following winter, but his fascinating diary of that tour shows his regret at being picked for only two Tests. In 1905/06 and 1913/14 he was more fortunate and played in ten Tests against South Africa, but his

only Test in England was the Second versus Australia in 1909, when he bowled 45 overs 15 maidens and took 5 for 85 in the first innings, but was then promptly dropped.

Statistics alone would give Albert Relf an important place in Sussex's history, but the man himself was also important. A smartly dressed man of dark complexion, with jet black hair and a luxurious moustache, he was loyal and conscientious and a perfect example to all the young professionals. His popularity, influence and strength of character made him an ideal coach and in New Zealand he guided Auckland to some success and also coached in India before returning to Wellington College to continue his father's work. He was deeply devoted to his wife, Agnes, and when she was taken seriously ill in 1937, he became greatly depressed; this clinical depression turned into mental illness and on Good Friday of that year the groundsman at Wellington found him in the pavilion shot through the heart. He died a relatively wealthy man; the tragic irony was that his wife later recovered from her operation.

# Robert R. Relf
*RHB & RMF, 1905-24*

**Born:** Sandhurst, Berkshire, 1 September 1883
**Died:** Reading, Berkshire, 28 April 1965

**Batting Record:**

| M | I | NO | Runs | Avge |
|---|---|----|------|------|
| 283 | 495 | 17 | 13,533 | 28.31 |
| **100** | **50** | | **CT/ST** | |
| 22 | 66 | | 282 | |

**Bowling Record:**

| O | M | Runs | W | Avge |
|---|---|------|---|------|
| 2,598 | 512 | 7,976 | 292 | 27.31 |
| **5wI** | **10wM** | | | |
| 11 | 1 | | | |

**Career Best Performances:**
272* v. Worcestershire, Eastbourne, 1909
42-10-79-8 v. Essex, Hove, 1910

Robert Relf played for his native Berkshire before qualifying for Sussex and making a disastrous debut against the Australians in 1905. But better things were in store: in the following season he became a regular member of the side and in 1907 he scored the first of his double hundreds when he saved the match against Kent at Canterbury by scoring 210 in the second innings. Legend has it that, prior to this innings, Charles Fry, preferring not to bat himself, had called rather peremptorily for 'Young Relf', now out of his whites, to don his pads as nightwatchman. Reaching the wicket, Robert conspired with Joe Vine to keep the great man waiting a little longer. Joe was not dismissed until 5.30 p.m. on the next day and Robert kept going after that!

One feature of his batsmanship was that, having reached a century, he often went on to the big hundreds that tend to win matches. He made 22 hundreds for Sussex and, although his career average is not outstanding, the average of his centuries (and not counting not out innings) is over 148. The following are examples of matches largely won by his big hundreds: in 1909 he scored 159 out of 344 against Nottinghamshire and later batted through the Sussex innings for an undefeated 272 out of 433 against Worcestershire. One year later in the Somerset match, *Wisden* praised his 'brilliant driving' as he put on 208 for the first wicket with Joe Vine and went on to reach 194 from a total of 465. In 1913, he took 177 out of 368 from the Oxford University bowlers after a partnership of 264 with Joe Vine.

Robert passed 1,000 runs in six seasons and also bowled effectively, going past 50 wickets in two seasons. After a poor 1919 season and not playing until July 1920, he promptly scored 225 against Lancashire, hitting 4 sixes, 1 five and 15 fours and thereby helping his side to an innings win. After 1921, when he had rattled up 193 out of 455 against Gloucestershire in another innings win by Sussex, his career seemed to tail off. Coming back in 1924 for the Surrey match, he was disqualified by having played for Berkshire in 1923.

But this was not the end of Robert Relf. He became a coach, and worked at Leighton Park School, Reading, between 1942 and 1960. This allowed him to continue playing Minor Counties cricket for Berkshire until he was sixty-three!

# Ian D.K. Salisbury
*RHB & LBG, 1989-96*

**Born:** Northampton, 21 January 1970

**County Cap:** 1991

**Batting Record:**

| M | I | NO | Runs | Avge |
|---|---|----|------|------|
| 129 | 168 | 38 | 2,450 | 18.85 |
| *127* | *83* | *23* | *775* | *12.92* |
| **100** | **50** | | CT/ST | |
| - | 6 | | 94 | |
| - | - | | *40* | |

**Bowling Record:**

| O | M | Runs | W | Avge |
|---|---|------|---|------|
| 4,159 | 973 | 13,078 | 381 | 34.35 |
| *948.3* | *49* | *4,243* | *124* | *34.22* |
| **5wl** | **10wM** | | | |
| 14 | 3 | | | |
| *1* | - | | | |

**Career Best performances:**
83 v. Glamorgan, Hove, 1996
*48* v. Glamorgan, Swansea, 1995 (SL)*
29.4-9-75-8 v. Essex, Chelmsford, 1996
*8-0-30-5 v. Leicestershire, Leicester, 1992 (SL)*

It was Paul Parker more than anyone else at Sussex who was interested in leg-spin bowling and his influence led, in 1988, to the acquisition of Andrew Clarke from Brighton club cricket. In virtually his one and only season he took 42 Championship wickets and did well in limited-overs matches, but he was essentially a 'roller' rather than a pure spinner and in 1989 the County took on Ian Salisbury who gave the ball a much firmer tweak. Raised in Northampton and attending a school where little cricket was played, Ian had rarely played the game until he was nearly fifteen. Then, when he was on the MCC groundstaff mainly as a batsman and seam bowler, he suddenly found that he could bowl some leg-breaks that were real 'jaffas'.

Although Ian's first three seasons were unflattering – 107 wickets at 46.80 – he started to come good in the 1992 season to such an extent that, besides topping the Sussex Championship averages with 79 wickets, he was also rewarded with two Test caps, becoming England's first specialist leg-spinner for twenty-one years. In his first match versus Pakistan at Lord's he bowled soundly in the first innings and in the second it appeared that he might be winning the match for England, but his skipper, Graham Gooch, opted for the quick men at a crucial moment and the chance was gone. From then on he enjoyed five England 'A' tours and two senior tours, but he was never able to establish himself fully. It was suspected that in Test cricket he bowled too many 'four balls', even for a leg-spinner, but at county level the story was often different. Leg-spinners can win matches for their side and Ian had at times enjoyed great success: his 7 for 54 (12 wickets in the match) saw Yorkshire off in 1992 and 7 for 72 and 8 for 75 in 1995 and 1996 respectively crushed Essex at Hove and at Chelmsford. It was ironic that he left his best until his last season with Sussex. After the County's poor season of 1996, he decided that he wanted to play for a side that would win some trophies and signed for Surrey. He enjoyed some success there too – including a further recall for England and a further senior tour – but what he forgot, sadly, was that he was the spin king at Hove, but number two to the Pakistani wizard, Saqlain Mushtaq, at The Oval.

# The Rt Rev. Lord David Sheppard

*RHB & SLA, 1947-62*

**Born:** Reigate, 6 March 1929

**County Cap:** 1949
**County Captain:** 1953

**Batting Record:**

| M | I | NO | Runs | Avge |
|---|---|----|------|------|
| 141 | 247 | 23 | 9,545 | 42.61 |
| **100** | **50** | | **CT/ST** | |
| 27 | 44 | | 123 | |

**Bowling Record:**

| O | M | Runs | W | Avge |
|---|---|------|---|------|
| 9 | 1 | 51 | 0 | — |
| **5wI** | **10wM** | | | |
| - | - | | | |

**Career Best Performances:**
204 v. Glamorgan, Eastbourne, 1949

Choices are never easy. David Sheppard might have been England captain for many years and would have ranked with May, Dexter and Cowdrey among the greatest amateur English batsmen of the post-war era. Instead he was, for a relatively short time, an excellent Test batsman and an inspiring county captain who became a bishop, a member of the House of Lords and a remarkable advocate for the under-privileged.

David came to prep school in Sussex before becoming a pupil at Sherborne School, where he had an outstanding record. In 1947, aged eighteen, he had his first match for Sussex – against Leicestershire – and was lbw first ball. After his National Service, he returned to the County in 1949 and played 11 matches, making over 900 runs, including 204 against Glamorgan and 147 against Leicestershire, joining John Langridge in an opening stand of 238 – some revenge for his first-ball duck two seasons previously. August saw the award of his county cap and October the start of study at Cambridge University. Much was expected of him and he did not disappoint. He passed 1,000 runs in the University season, scored 4 hundreds, including 227 in an opening partnership of 343 with John Dewes against the West Indians at Fenner's.

This innings doubtless prompted the England selectors to call him up for the Fourth Test at the Oval. He ended his first full season 15 runs short of 1,900.

David's 1951 and 1952 seasons proved to be equally successful and in the second of these he headed the national batting averages, scoring nearly 2,300 runs with 10 hundreds, including the highest score of his career – 239 not out for Cambridge against Worcestershire. Although he was a member of the 1950/51 MCC side to tour Australia and played in two Tests, he did not find himself back in England colours until the Third and Fourth Tests against India in 1952, when he scored his first Test hundred, 119 at The Oval.

In 1953, having decided to take Holy Orders, he agreed to take over the Sussex captaincy in a side which appeared ready to fulfil its potential. They made an indifferent start, but in June and July Sussex were leading the Championship table; too many drawn matches later in the season, however, meant that they had to cede first place to the powerful Surrey side. David himself scored over 2,000 runs with 7 hundreds, but did not add to his Test caps. For the County, however, he proved to be an inspirational leader, lifting the players by his personal example and encouragement on and off the field. In 1954, he continued to play fairly

*David Sheppard, Bishop of Liverpool, (right) accompanied by Mike Brearley, attends Central Hall, Westminster, to engage in debate over the proposed MCC tour to South Africa in 1983.*

regularly under Hubert Doggart's leadership, but owing to his pastoral duties his appearances became increasingly spasmodic, although his final match was not until 1962.

That he kept himself in form with some matches for Sussex meant he remained a candidate for England sides and, when Len Hutton was unfit for the Second and Third Tests against Pakistan in 1954, he was called in to lead the side and open the batting. It was even mooted at the time that he was the right man to take the MCC side to Australasia in 1954/55, but the task fell eventually to Hutton. He was little involved in cricket in 1955, but when the Australians came to England in the following summer he was recalled by England for the Fourth (Laker's great match) and Fifth Tests and scored 113 at Old Trafford, becoming the first ordained priest to play Test cricket. His England career now appeared to be over and in the late 1950s he found little time to play even for Sussex. 1962 saw him again playing rather more and a century for the Gentlemen led to his inclusion in the 1962/63 tour of Australia and New Zealand, led by Ted Dexter of Sussex, when he scored over 1,000 first class runs, played in another 8 Tests and made 113 at Melbourne. But that was really his swansong. His had been a remarkable career: his ability to make runs on important occasions and score big hundreds when not always in regular practice was an indication of his meticulous attention to technique and his massive powers of concentration. He was, perhaps, slightly less endowed with natural ability than some of his great contemporaries, but he made himself into a commanding presence as an opening batsman and a splendid close fielder.

In the period 1957-69 he was Warden of the Mayflower Family Centre in London's East End. He was then Bishop of Woolwich before becoming Bishop of Liverpool in 1975. His deep social concern and his remarkable rapport with his Roman Catholic counterpart made a lasting impression on the life of the city. Cricket's loss was certainly the Church's gain and his achievements on and off the field have encouraged wide respect and admiration.

99

# Sir C. Aubrey Smith

*RHB & RF, 1882-96*

**Born:** City of London, 21 July 1863
**Died:** Beverly Hills, California, 20 December 1948

**County Captain:** 1887-1888, 1890

**Batting Record:**

| M | I | NO | Runs | Avge |
|---|---|----|------|------|
| 99 | 175 | 16 | 2,315 | 14.55 |
| 100 | 50 | | CT/ST | |
| - | 8 | | 51 | |

**Bowling Record:**

| O | M | Runs | W | Avge |
|---|---|------|---|------|
| 2,539 | 1,021 | 5,006 | 208 | 24.06 |
| 5wI | 10wM | | | |
| 13 | 1 | | | |

**Career Best Performances:**
85 v. Gloucestershire, Hove, 1888
12-4-16-7 v. MCC, Lord's, 1890
(5 balls to the over)

Sir C. Aubrey Smith is best remembered as a film star portraying the typical English gentleman and few realise that, in his younger days, he was the Sussex captain – and, for one match, the England captain too – and was considered to be one of the best association football forwards of his day.

Charles Aubrey Smith was the son of Dr C.J. Smith, a Brighton doctor, and was educated at Charterhouse and Cambridge University, where he won a blue in each of his four years. He started playing for Sussex in 1882 while still at Cambridge and played with varying regularity until 1896. He led the side in three seasons when the County was not particularly strong and, in two of these seasons – 1888 and 1890 – they finished last in the Championship. Aubrey was over 6ft tall, bowled fast round-arm and his unusual run-up led to his being known as 'Round the Corner' Smith. He apparently started his run-up on some occasions from a deep mid-off position and on others from behind the umpire, causing Dr W.G. Grace to remark: 'It is rather startling when he suddenly appears at the bowling crease.' Among his best performances for Sussex

were 5 for 8 versus his old university in 1885 and 7 for 16 versus MCC in 1890. He was also a hard-hitting batsman who never scored a first-class century, but made 142 in a second-class match against Hampshire in 1888.

He toured Australia in the winter of 1887/88 and captained an England side which went to South Africa in the following winter. He played in the First Test against South Africa at Port Elizabeth and became the only player to captain England on his sole appearance in Test cricket. He remained for a while in South Africa as a stockbroker and played for Transvaal before returning to this country to start a career on the stage, firstly in Hastings in 1892 and then in London in 1895. He acted on the London and New York stages for some thirty years before being cast in 1931 by MGM in the film *The Bachelor Father*. This was a turning point in his career, albeit at a relatively advanced age, because he then settled in Hollywood and made further films. He founded a cricket club there which he captained, lived in a house named 'The Round Corner' and was knighted in 1944 for services to Anglo-American friendship.

# Charles L.A. Smith
*RHB & RMF, 1898-1911*

**Born:** Henfield, 1 January 1879
**Died:** Wineham, near Henfield, 22 November 1949

**County Captain:** 1906 and 1909

**Batting Record:**

| M | I | NO | Runs | Avge |
|---|---|----|------|------|
| 218 | 332 | 36 | 5,788 | 19.55 |
| **100** | **50** | | **CT/ST** | |
| 2 | 23 | | 147 | |

**Bowling Record:**

| O | M | Runs | W | Avge |
|---|---|------|---|------|
| 152 | 25 | 585 | 9 | 65.00 |

(5 or 6 balls to the over)

**Career Best Performances:**
103* v  Kent, Hove, 1902
103* v. Lancashire, Hove, 1906
1-1-0-1 v. Surrey, Oval, 1898

C.L.A. SMITH.

Sir C. Aubrey Smith and Charles Smith were not related, but Charles came from an old Sussex cricketing family, his father, C.H. Smith, having played for the County between 1861 and 1874, often as captain. In the 1890s Charles attended Brighton College, where he was an outstanding batsman and a useful fast bowler who captured 166 wickets at 16 runs each during his seasons there, although he rarely bowled once he went into county cricket. He first played for Sussex, aged nineteen, in 1898 and, in the July of that year, he played a prominent part in an interesting match with Surrey. Sussex, having been set 305 to win, appeared to be cruising to victory at 193 for 4 wickets, but then wickets began to fall quickly and, although Charles batted well for 78 not out, he could find nobody to stay with him and the County were dismissed for 231. The *Daily Telegraph* commented that 'it was a very trying experience for a schoolboy to do so well in a big county match and to find half a dozen professionals unable to get more than twenty runs between them'.

At the start of an innings Charles often appeared cramped and uncertain, but once set he was a stylish hard-hitting batsman. In 1902, having established himself in the county side, he made 103 not out against Kent and joined George Brann (126*) in an unbroken eighth wicket partnership of 229, a record which has endured to this day. In the second match of the 1906 season, C.B. Fry was injured and Charles took over the captaincy for the remainder of the season and scored over 1,000 runs and the second of his two centuries – both exactly the same score, 103 not out – against Lancashire. In 1909, when C.B. Fry had decided to play for Hampshire owing to his duties on *TS Mercury*, he again took over the captaincy and led the County to fourth place in the Championship. In this season, too, he was associated in another unbroken eighth wicket partnership – on this occasion against Derbyshire. Charles made an unbeaten 66 and with George Leach (113*) he added 179 in eighty minutes. Although Sussex had done so well in 1909 after some poor results in 1906 and 1907 and Charles had shown himself to be not only an able leader, but a popular one too, he did not continue in the following season and handed over the reins to Herbert Chaplin.

# David M. Smith
*LHB & RMF, 1989-94*

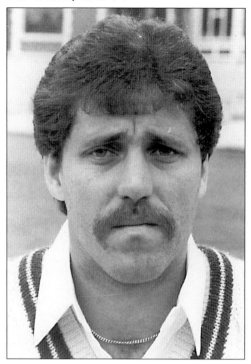

**Born:** Balham, London, 9 January 1956

**County Cap:** 1989

**Batting Record:**

| M | I | NO | Runs | Avge |
|---|---|----|------|------|
| 89 | 156 | 20 | 5,100 | 37.50 |
| *68* | *67* | *4* | *2,364* | *37.52* |

| 100 | 50 | | CT/ST | |
|-----|----|--|-------|--|
| 9 | 28 | | 62 | |
| *3* | *16* | | *22* | |

**Bowling Record:**

| O | M | Runs | W | Avge |
|---|---|------|---|------|
| 10 | 0 | 54 | 0 | -- |

| 5wI | 10wM |
|-----|------|
| - | - |

**Career Best Performances:**
213 v. Essex, Southend, 1992
*124 v. Warwickshire, Lord's, 1993 (NWT Final)*

Sussex was David Smith's last port of call in a varied and eventful cricket career and his contribution to the County's cricket over his six seasons was by no means negligible.

Aged seventeen, he began his career with Surrey in 1973 and appeared a most promising player, even if somewhat prone to injury and a little temperamental. He did not, however, make the expected impact and it was only in 1982 that he passed 1,000 Championship runs. In 1984, he moved to Worcestershire and scored 1,000 Championship runs in each of his three seasons, averaging nearly 44. With his powerful frame and his determined attitude gained at his new county, he became known as one of the country's best players of pace, which was exemplified in 1985 by his 112 and 87 at Portsmouth in face of some ferocious bowling by Malcolm Marshall of Hampshire. As a result he found himself selected for the England side, led by David Gower, which toured West Indies in 1985/86. England were, of course, 'blackwashed' in this series, but David top-scored in both innings of the Fourth Test with 47 and 32. The 1987 and 1988 seasons saw him back at Surrey, before

his final move to Sussex in 1989. In the following winter he was again summoned to the West Indies – to replace Graham Gooch, who had suffered a broken hand – but had his own thumb broken in his only innings.

David took to Sussex very easily, passing 1,000 runs in three of his first four seasons and failing to do so only in 1990 when a broken thumb again sidelined him. Big hundreds have always won matches and he was often able to convert an ordinary hundred into a large score. In his first season he made 184 against Nottinghamshire, and in 1992 he took 213 off the Essex attack. Perhaps his outstanding contribution to Sussex was, however, his 124 run out in the 1993 NatWest final against Warwickshire. He batted throughout the Sussex innings of 321 for 6 wickets, which Warwickshire overhauled off the very last ball. It was a heart-breaking result for Sussex, but it remains the greatest limited-overs final played so far. Had David completed his final run, the result could have been so very different.

At the end of the 1994 season, David retired from first-class cricket to become Second XI captain and batting coach, a post which he held for just the one year before becoming the victim of re-organisation.

# Donald V. Smith
## LHB & LM, 1946-62

**Born:** Broadwater, 14 June 1923

**County Cap:** 1950

**Batting Record:**

| M | I | NO | Runs | Avge |
|---|---|----|------|------|
| 360 | 596 | 63 | 15,935 | 29.89 |
| **100** | **50** | | **CT/ST** | |
| 17 | 84 | | 220 | |

**Bowling Record:**

| O | M | Runs | W | Avge |
|---|---|------|---|------|
| 3,408 | 996 | 8,928 | 308 | 28.99 |
| **5wI** | **10wM** | | | |
| 5 | 1 | | | |

**Career Best Performances:**
206* v. Nottinghamshire, Trent Bridge 1950
19-9-29-6 v. Glamorgan, Hove, 1956

Don Smith's career had some unusual aspects to it. He was probably the first man from Worthing ever to win an England Test cap at cricket, he played an innings at Hove which came as near to Alletson's as that of anyone past or present, and in mid-career he suddenly became a very useful bowler.

He joined the Sussex staff in 1946. For three seasons he produced nothing extraordinary, but in 1949 he began to open the innings with John Langridge and in the following year took it on full time. His maiden hundred was a double ton against Nottinghamshire, which included 3 sixes and 28 fours. In this excellent season he passed 1,500 runs and looked set for a long stint as an opener, but he then found himself relegated when David Sheppard came down from university. It was a sad fact of life in Sussex cricket in the 1950s that their brilliant amateurs appeared half-way through the season and ousted the somewhat less able professionals.

From 1951 to 1954, Don was mainly the third opener, but in 1955 he was back at the top of the order and in that year Robin Marlar, the new skipper, suggested that he try bowling left-arm medium over the wicket. Prior to that time he had taken 9 wickets in nine seasons, and now he bowled over 650 overs and took 73 wickets at just over 18 each. From then on he continued to make a sound contribution to the County's bowling, but 1957 was his real *annus mirabilis*. Things got off to a good start when he played a devastating innings against Gloucestershire at Hove. The County were set to get 277 runs in 195 minutes and Don flayed the visitors' attack to the tune of 166 with 9 sixes and 11 fours in less than three hours. It was not quite Alletson, but it was marvellous stuff. A few weeks later he took an unbeaten 147 off the West Indians and found himself suddenly called up to open for England. His three Tests, sadly, were not successful, but it was a marvellous summer with a total of over 2,000 runs in all matches.

Don passed 1,000 runs in four of his last five seasons before retiring at the end of 1962. He had plenty to do: he had been always known as a Sussex soccer referee and he began coaching cricket at Lancing College. In 1984 he became Sri Lanka's team manager, before emigrating to Australia a year later.

# John A. Snow
*RHB & RF, 1961-77*

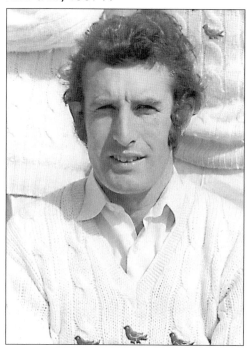

**Born:** Peopleton, Worcestershire, 13 October 1941

**County Cap:** 1964

**Batting Record:**

| M | I | NO | Runs | Avge |
|---|---|----|------|------|
| 267 | 350 | 88 | 3,828 | 14.61 |
| *160* | *121* | *32* | *1,070* | *12.02* |

| 100 | 50 | CT/ST | |
|-----|----|----|----|
| - | 9 | 104 | |
| - | *2* | *33* | |

**Bowling Record:**

| O | M | Runs | W | Avge |
|---|---|------|---|------|
| 7,199 | 1,644 | 18,789 | 883 | 21.27 |
| *1,297.1* | *180* | *4,256* | *223* | *19.09* |

| 5wI | 10wM |
|-----|------|
| 46 | 8 |
| *2* | - |

**Career Best Performances:**
73* v. Worcestershire, Worcester 1977
*57 v. Lancashire, Horsham, 1977 (SL)*
27-1-87-8 v. Middlesex, Lord's, 1975
*7.5-1-15-5 v. Surrey, Hove, 1972 (SL)*

Something of an *enfant terrible* at times in his career, the despair of some captains and an enigmatic character even to those who thought they knew him well, John Snow is nevertheless rightly regarded as among the greatest of post-war English fast bowlers, a powerful and hostile match-winner on his day. Born in Worcestershire, he came to Sussex when his father, a vicar, took over a Bognor Regis parish, which led to his attending Christ's Hospital School in Horsham. He was recommended initially to the County as a batsman and in his second match for Sussex in 1961 he scored 15 and 35, both not out, although the fact that he could bowl had also been recognised. His action may not have been classical, but his long, loping relaxed strides created a beautiful rhythm.

Although his chances were strictly limited in his first two years, he came to the fore in 1963 to such an extent that, while playing only twelve Championship matches, he found himself included in the team to play the first limited-overs final at Lord's and in the course of eight overs he took 3 for 13 in the County's win over Worcestershire. This led, of course, to his inclusion in the one-day side in the following year when the County successfully defended

their title. 77 wickets in 1964 and 100 in 1965 were sufficient evidence of his ability for the England selectors to call him into the team for two Tests against New Zealand and South Africa in the latter year. From 1966, a season in which he took 114 wickets for the County and headed the bowling for a second successive year, he became a regular in the England side and, at the same time, began to show that the initial promise of his batting was not a fiction, as he scored a maiden 50 for the County. Furthermore, in the final Test against West Indies at the Oval, he partnered Ken Higgs of Lancashire in a last-wicket stand of 128 in which his own share was 59. The demands of Test cricket, however, limited his appearances for the County in the late 1960s and early 1970s and, although he did not reach 100 wickets again in a season, he continued to knock over countless county batsmen, often at a cost of fewer than 20 runs per wicket.

His deeds for England at this time were legion and quite remarkable. On the tour of the West

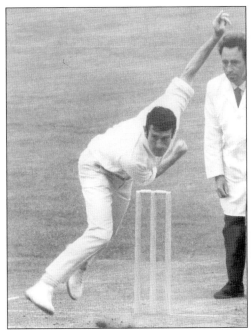

Left: *John Snow bowls for England v. Australia in the Third Test at Edgbaston in 1968.* Right: *Mulling over with Mike Griffith the County's 5-run win over Middlesex in the Gillette Cup semi-final at Lord's in 1973.*

Indies in 1967/68 – a series which England won by 1-0 – he took 27 wickets in the four Tests in which he played, including 7 for 49 at Sabina Park in the second match. Returning to this country for the 1968 season, when the visitors were the Australians, he took a further 17 wickets and in 1970/71 he was one of the principal reasons why England under Ray Illingworth regained the Ashes for England. His 7 for 40 in the Third Test of this six-match series saw Australia bundled out for 116 in their second innings at Sydney and England win by the massive margin of 299 runs. Although he was dropped by England for some series in the first half of the 1970s, he was usually recalled when the going became tough, and he took 24 wickets against the 1972 Australians and 15 in three matches against the 1976 West Indians. Of his 202 Test wickets, 83 were claimed against Australia and 72 against the West Indies. In all, John played 49 Tests for England and in only one of these matches did he fail to take a wicket.

Success can, however, have its downside, as some England players find nowadays when it comes to relationships with their counties. In

the 1971 season, after John had captured only 3 wickets for 223 runs in three matches, the Sussex committee decided to drop him, commenting that 'his bowling performances, and more especially his fielding, have been so lacking in effort that the selection committee had no alternative'. He wisely accepted the criticism, but pointed out that his efforts for England had taken a toll and, after a month's absence, he came back to the side, taking 11 wickets in a win over Essex and receiving a recall by England. Sadly, this did not lead to a happy outcome, for in the First Test against India at Lord's, in which he top-scored for England with 73, he managed to barge Indian opener Sunil Gavaskar and was dropped for the second match on disciplinary grounds.

John left the Sussex scene in 1977, published two volumes of poetry and, after playing some Sunday League matches for Warwickshire in 1980, he retired to found his own travel business specialising in cricket tours. Nowadays he supports Sussex in a different role – as a member of their committee, of which he is now vice-chairman.

# James Southerton

*RHB & SRA, 1858-72*

**Born:** Petworth, 16 November 1827
**Died:** Mitcham Green, Surrey, 16 June 1880

**Batting Record:**

| M | I | NO | Runs | Avge |
|---|---|----|------|------|
| 50 | 83 | 14 | 613 | 8.88 |
| 100 | 50 | | CT/ST | |
| - | 2 | | 43 | |

**Bowling Record:**

| Runs | W | Avge |
|------|---|------|
| 3,525 | 269 | 13.10 |
| 5wl | 10wM | |
| 32 | 15 | |

**Career Best performances:**
53 v. Kent, Tunbridge Wells, 1858
8-68 v. Lancashire, Old Trafford, 1869

James Southerton was something of a rolling stone. Born in Sussex, he spent some of his youth in Lincolnshire before coming to live at Mitcham in Surrey. In 1854, he made his first-class debut by virtue of his residential qualification for Surrey against Sussex, the county of his birth. In 1858, he was claimed by Sussex and from then until 1872 he was usually regarded as a Sussex player, if required, whenever a conflict of loyalties arose. After a dispute with Sussex in 1861, he moved to Southampton as an employee of Hampshire CCC, and either played for them or for Sussex and, if not required for either, for Surrey. In 1867, this anomalous situation reached a peak when he played for all three counties in the one season! He then left Hampshire and returned to Mitcham, but did not play regularly for Surrey until after 1872.

Little more than 5ft 6in tall and relatively light, he grew mutton-chop whiskers to compensate for an early onset of baldness. He was known as a cheerful and courteous man of complete honesty. At the start of his career he was regarded as something of a 'bits and pieces' cricketer and, although he started playing aged twenty-six, it was not until he was into his late thirties that he was taken seriously as a bowler. The MCC's 1864 amendment to Law X allowed the bowler's arm to rise above the shoulder and this seemed to transform his ability. In 1867, he captured 132 wickets (average 14.14) for his three counties. Few players have had to wait until their fortieth year to make an impression on the game. Although he had written an essay, 'A Few Wrinkles on Bowling' in which he had spoken of the arm being kept level with the shoulder, there is no doubt that he did not wholly practise what he preached. The off-break – popular belief was that he could 'turn it a yard' – was his chief weapon and for a few years, before the emergence of Alfred Shaw, he reigned supreme in this department, his best season for Sussex being 1870, when he took 210 first-class wickets.

Playing on until 1879, albeit with Surrey, when he was by then fifty-one, he attracted the sobriquet of 'The Evergreen' and on the England tour to Australia in 1876/77 he played in the first two Test matches against Australia, making his debut at the age of forty-nine, a record that is most unlikely to be broken.

# John Spencer

RHB & RMF, 1969-80

**Born:** Brighton, 6 October 1949

**County Cap:** 1973

**Batting Record:**

| M | I | NO | Runs | Avge |
|---|---|----|------|------|
| 186 | 243 | 64 | 2,457 | 13.72 |
| 186 | 89 | 42 | 411 | 8.74 |

| 100 | 50 | | CT/ST |
|-----|----|--|-------|
| - | 5 | | 64 |
| - | - | | 39 |

**Bowling Record:**

| O | M | Runs | W | Avge |
|---|---|------|---|------|
| 4,877 | 1,242 | 12,599 | 464 | 27.15 |
| 1,494.1 | 198 | 5,175 | 220 | 23.52 |

**Career Best performances:**
79 v. Hampshire, Southampton, 1975
*35 v. Northamptonshire, Northampton, 1977 (SL)*
14.3-6-19-6 v. Gloucestershire, Gloucester, 1974
*8-1-16-4 v. Somerset, Hove, 1973 (SL)*

John Spencer is Sussex through and through. Educated at the Brighton, Hove and Sussex Grammar School, he first played for the County, aged nineteen, in 1969 and took 20 wickets in six matches. In the same autumn he took up a place at Cambridge and won a blue in each of his three seasons there, heading the bowling in his second and third years; his 30 wickets in his last year cost no more than 14.56 runs each. In that year, he played a decisive part in his university's comprehensive innings victory over Oxford by bowling 33 overs, 15 maidens and taking 7 wickets for 57 in the two innings. While at university he played for Sussex in the vacations and in 1970 he was good enough to play for Sussex in the Gillette Cup final.

On leaving Cambridge, he devoted himself to the County and from 1973 until 1979 he was part and parcel of the attack in both first-class and limited-overs cricket. In its report for the 1974 season, *Wisden* noted that 'another gratifying aspect was the continued improvement of Spencer in his role of stock bowler'. A season later he reached 56 first-class wickets and he was the most economical bowler nationally in the John Player Sunday League, with 19 wickets (average 17.94) and 2.92 runs per over. His long-handled batting was also showing results and he amassed more than 500 runs in both 1975 and 1976. In the first of these two seasons, Sussex were forced to follow on against Hampshire, but saved the game in fine style with Mark Faber contributing 176 and John scoring 79 in 25 minutes and on course for the fastest hundred of the season, albeit in part against some occasional bowlers. In 1975, *Wisden* was even more effusive: 'Spencer proved steady and a bowler with the ability to swing the ball in a most disconcerting manner. He is a most enthusiastic player and non-stop worker, forging away to remind spectators of Maurice Tate and, in post-war years, of Ian Thomson's willing toil.'

Towards the end of the 1970s, Sussex's quick bowling was mainly in the hands of Imran, Garth le Roux and Geoff Arnold, and John's chances became more limited and his form, therefore, less good. Consequently, after 1980 he decided to accept a post at Brighton College, where amongst his duties has been the coaching of cricket – his charges included, of course, Neil Lenham. Definitely Sussex through and through!

# George B. Street
*RHB & WK, 1909-23*

**Born:** Charlwood, Surrey, 6 December 1889
**Died:** Portslade, 24 April 1924

**Batting Record:**

| M | I | NO | Runs | Avge |
|---|---|---|---|---|
| 192 | 296 | 70 | 3,781 | 16.73 |
| **100** | **50** | | **CT/ST** | |
| 1 | 11 | | 304/116 | |

**Bowling Record:**

| O | M | Runs | W | Avge |
|---|---|---|---|---|
| 17 | 2 | 66 | 3 | 22.00 |
| **5wI** | **10wM** | | | |
| - | - | | | |

**Career Best Performances:**
109 v. Essex, Colchester, 1921
7.3-2-26-3 v. Warwickshire, Nuneaton, 1914
Best season 1923: 95 dismissals (ct 69, st 26)

Kent, so it is said, produce the great wicketkeepers, but in the first half of the twentieth century Sussex also took their share. When the successful Harry Butt retired in 1912, he was succeeded by George Street, who came to be considered by many to be as good a 'keeper as any in England in the early 1920s. He was also only the sixth regular Sussex 'keeper since 1817, a successor to William Broadbridge, Tom Box, C.H. Ellis, Harry Phillips and Harry Butt.

George, aged nineteen, joined Sussex in 1909, but there were three years of apprenticeship before he took over the gloves from Butt in 1913. Assured of his place, he did especially well in the next season, claiming 58 catches and 15 stumpings.

With the resumption of cricket in 1919, Sussex had to make do with a rag-bag selection of wicketkeepers, with at least one professional and four amateurs doing the job, the best known of the amateurs being the Eton schoolmaster, Richard Young. By 1920, George was coming into his prime and took 5 dismissals in an

innings on five occasions in that season and those following, and claiming 7 catches and one stumping in the match against Worcestershire at Hastings in 1923. His contribution as a middle-order batsman was not negligible either, as he scored over 800 runs in 1921 and 1922 and took 109 off the Essex bowling at Colchester in 1921.

In 1922/23, the MCC side under F.T. Mann was touring South Africa and when the Hampshire 'keeper, Walter Livsey, was injured, George was summoned to replace him and he played in his one Test match at Durban.

The 1922 *Wisden*, in its comments on Sussex for the season ahead, remarked: 'Street is young and has plenty of time before him.' After his successful season in 1923 and with all unhappy thoughts of his replacement by Richard Young in the latter part of the 1922 season banished – Young was not the better keeper at all, but perceived as a more productive batsman – George was looking forward to the 1924 season. At a practice in April he had been discussing his further England prospects with his County captain, Arthur Gilligan, who was, in fact, to captain the MCC side to Australia in the following winter. Then, riding his motorcycle home to Warnham and attempting to avoid a lorry at Portslade, he crashed into a wall and was killed instantly. How tragically incorrect *Wisden* had proved to be.

# Kenneth G. Suttle

*LHB & SLA, 1949-71*

**Born:** Brook Green, Kensington, London, 25 August 1928

**Batting Record:**

| M | I | NO | Runs | Avge |
|---|---|---|---|---|
| 601 | 1043 | 91 | 29,375 | 30.85 |
| *53* | *50* | *4* | *1,007* | *21.89* |

| 100 | 50 | | CT/ST | |
|---|---|---|---|---|
| 49 | 147 | | 376/2 | |
| *2* | *3* | | *10* | |

**Bowling Record:**

| O | M | Runs | W | Avge |
|---|---|---|---|---|
| 3,469 | 1,111 | 8,590 | 260 | 33.03 |
| *123* | *21* | *451* | *16* | *28.19* |

**Career Best Performances:**
204* v. Kent, Tunbridge Wells, 1962
*104 v. Kent, Tunbridge Wells, 1963 (GC)*
23-8-64-6 v. Worcestershire, Worcester, 1970
*7-3-24-4 v. Northamptonshire, Kettering, 1970 (SL)*

Ken Suttle's family moved from London to Worthing when he was nine, so he can quite easily claim a real Sussex background. After National Service in the Parachute Regiment, he played and scored heavily in Worthing club cricket before joining the County in 1949. He was capped in 1952 and from August 1954 until June 1969 he played an incredible 423 consecutive County Championship matches – he was almost literally a permanent fixture in the County team over a very long period. His left-hand batting was crisp and attractive, while he was also a slow left-arm bowler, an outstanding fielder who threw on the turn (a rare ability in pre-one-day cricket) and, if the need arose, a reserve wicketkeeper. Small in stature, he was strong and always fit as he played soccer as a left-wing for Worthing, Tonbridge, Brighton and Chelsea and, finally, player-manager at Arundel. His fitness record in the wear and tear of constant sport was remarkable and compares well with that of some contemporary players.

Ken can be compared in some respects with his predecessor, John Langridge. They both scored 1,000 runs in a season seventeen times – Ken's 2,326, (average 39.42) in 1962, including his one double hundred, being his best year – and they both should have played for England. John's tour to India in 1939/40 was aborted owing to the Second World War, but Ken was lucky enough to be selected for the 1953/54 tour of the West Indies. Although he was seen in some quarters as England's answer to Australia's Neil Harvey, he did not play in a Test. Prior to the Second Test on the tour he had just made 96 and 62 against Barbados, but the number six slot was given to the tour manager, Charles Palmer, and Ken became a permanent twelfth man. Had he been picked at that point and with the later development of limited-overs cricket, in which he performed most creditably for Sussex, there is a strong possibility that some form of international recognition would have come his way. Confining himself, therefore, to county cricket, he continued to score heavily, glancing and cutting especially well, not always following the rules of the text book, but usually extricating himself with the speed of his foot movement. It is worth noting that his record of 29,375 runs for the County has been exceeded only by John Langridge.

In the course of his career Ken was involved

*Ken Suttle* (left) *cuts Fred Titmus to the boundary in the course of his 149\* for Sussex v. Middlesex at Lord's in 1967.*

in 90 century partnerships, one of the most remarkable being the 119 for the 9th wicket against Worcestershire at Eastbourne when Ken scored 109 of the runs added and his partner, P.A. Kelland, a mere 5. He scored a hundred against every county (something that even John Langridge failed to do) and twice carried his bat throughout an innings. In 1964, he was unbeaten on 97 out of the County's total of 164 against Lancashire at Liverpool. Two years later, at Grace Road, Leicester, he was on the field for the whole seventeen and a half hours of the match, scoring 89 not out of the first innings total of 161 and 139 not out from 265 for 2 wickets in the second. If one adds in 43 overs, 17 maidens and 3 wickets for 67 and, for good measure, a catch, it was a truly remarkable all-round performance. As a bowler, Ken did not take a first-class wicket in his first seven seasons, but after the 1956 season, when he headed the County's bowling averages with 24 wickets at 16.75 each, he continued to bowl regularly, taking 4 for 6 against Lancashire in 1959 and 4 for 5 against Worcestershire two years later, but

not producing his best analysis until 1970 when he was a month off his forty-second birthday.

While his statistical contribution to Sussex is sufficient to mark him down for a prominent position in the club's history, there is much more to say about him. His friendly disposition, his perky walk, his chatter to his friend, the 6ft 5in Alan Oakman who towered above Ken as they walked down to the other end when over was called, his mischievous grin and his sense of fun – all this endeared him to the team and members alike. The manner of his leaving Sussex leaves a black mark against the County's staff relations. In 1971 he appeared at the ground expecting to play and was told that he would not be needed – ever again. In fact, he did play a few more games that season because a joint benefit with Jim Parks had been arranged for the next season. So he was required to remain in Sussex for 1972, but he was relegated to Second XI matches. It seems incredible, but is true – a shoddy end to magnificent service, and so reminiscent of the treatment meted out to Maurice Tate a generation before.

# Frederick W. Tate

*RHB & RSM, 1887-1905*

**Born:** Brighton, 24 July 1867
**Died:** Burgess Hill, 24 February 1943

**Batting Record:**

| M | I | NO | Runs | Avge |
|---|---|----|------|------|
| 312 | 444 | 144 | 2,876 | 9.58 |

| 100 | 50 | | CT/ST | |
|-----|----|--|-------|--|
| - | 6 | | 230 | |

**Bowling Record:**

| O | M | Runs | W | Avge |
|---|---|------|---|------|
| 12,438 | 4,024 | 28,054 | 1,306 | 21.48 |

| 5wI | 10wM | | | |
|-----|------|--|--|--|
| 103 | 29 | | | |

**Career Best Performances:**
84 v. Nottinghamshire, Hove, 1901
41.3-15-73-9 v. Leicestershire, Leicester, 1902

Fred Tate, father of Maurice and often known as 'Chub', is probably better remembered in cricket history for his dropped catch at Old Trafford in 1902 than for his sterling bowling for Sussex over eighteen seasons.

Fred came on to the Sussex staff in 1887 and, one year later in the match against Kent at Tonbridge, the home side, needing only 45 runs to win and coasting at 41 for 4 wickets, were ambushed by Fred who took 5 wickets for 1 run, so that they finally scraped home by one wicket. He bowled off-breaks at rather below medium pace and was capable of prodigiously long spells without loss of accuracy, relying on a lively pace off the pitch rather than a long run. It was said 'that Tate clean bowls more first-class bats on perfect wickets than any other medium pace bowler.' He was not an outstanding batsman, but fielded well in the slips.

His first 100-wicket haul in a season was in 1897 and he repeated the feat in four more seasons, 1902 being his best year when he claimed 161 wickets (average 14.92), including a match analysis of 15 wickets for 68 runs against Middlesex. In 1891, he bowled 9.3 overs with 5 maidens and took 7 wickets for 7 runs against Oxford University, while he did the hat-trick against Surrey in 1901 and took 3 wickets in 4 balls against Nottinghamshire in 1902.

In 1902, on his thirty-fifth birthday, he made his Test debut for England against Australia at Old Trafford. England, 27 runs behind on the first innings, were making inroads into the Australian batting in the second knock. A.C. MacLaren had moved Fred from his usual position at slip to the leg boundary and Joe Darling struck a skyer to him which he dropped. Australia would have been 10 for 4, but recovered to 86 all out. England, needing 124 to win, collapsed to 116 for 9 when Fred came to the wicket. After a break for rain, he scored 4 of the runs needed, but was then bowled. England lost by three runs and Fred seems to have taken the blame for their failure to square the series. It is said that, going home to Haywards Heath, he confessed to his friend Len Braund, from whose bowling the catch had been missed: 'I've got a little kid at home there who'll make up for it to me.' How right his prediction proved to be!

# Maurice W. Tate
*RHB & OB/RFM, 1912-37*

**Born:** Brighton, 30 May 1895
**Died:** Wadhurst, Sussex, 18 May 1956

**Batting Record:**

| M | I | NO | Runs | Avge |
|---|---|----|------|------|
| 525 | 774 | 72 | 17,076 | 24.32 |

| 100 | 50 | | CT/ST | |
|-----|-----|--|-------|--|
| 18 | 68 | | 226 | |

**Bowling Record:**

| O | M | Runs | W | Avge |
|---|---|------|---|------|
| 19,485 | 5,689 | 38,515 | 2,211 | 17.41 |

| 5wI | 10wM |
|-----|------|
| 159 | 38 |

**Career Best Performances:**
203 v. Northamptonshire, Hove, 1921
39.1-12-71-9 v. Middlesex, Lord's, 1926

The Sussex *aficionados* always assert, with considerable justification, that Maurice Tate was the County's greatest cricketer, not, of course, the greatest batsman, although an excellent one, but certainly the greatest bowler. His father, Fred or 'Chub' (a sobriquet handed on to Maurice), forever associated with the dropped catch against Australia in 1902, hoped that his son would redeem his blunder, although this apparent millstone did not ever appear to upset Maurice. A large, amiable man with a broad grin and large feet, he was a gift to contemporary cartoonists.

His Sussex career began in 1912 when he bowled off-breaks, not dissimilar from those of his father, and, although the first three seasons after the First World War brought him some reasonable success as a bowler, it was not until 1922 that his real ability came to the fore. When this transformation occurred is disputed. John Arlott, in an appreciation, asserts that the moment occurred when, in late July at Eastbourne, his faster ball castled Phil Mead, as near an 'unbowlable' batsman as there then was, but Arthur Gilligan, Maurice's county captain, believes that it occurred rather earlier that year. Sussex had been to Hull and had been dismissed

by Yorkshire for 20 in their second innings and the spare day resulted in net practice. Having bowled a few off-breaks at his skipper he suddenly produced a faster ball which spreadeagled the stumps. This happened twice more in succession and Arthur decided that Maurice needed to quicken his pace. In the very next match – against Kent at Tunbridge Wells – he was almost unplayable, taking 3 wickets in 4 balls and 8 for 67 in their first innings. His run-up was a mere eight paces and a well-nigh perfect action produced either late swerve from leg or a ball that came back from outside the off-stump. What is more, it seemed as if the ball gained pace off the pitch. In the Test trial in 1923, he took 5 wickets without a run being scored from him as the Rest plummeted from 200 for 4 to 205 all out. It was no surprise that in 1924 he found himself in England's team and, on his debut, he and Arthur Gilligan bowled South Africa out for 30, his own share being 4 for 12.

The three seasons of 1923 until 1925 were quite remarkable. For the County he took 527 wickets (average 13.07) and in all matches, including Tests, 771, over 200 in each of the three seasons. Inevitably, he was selected to tour Australia in 1924/25 under Arthur Gilligan's leadership and, in the five Tests, he took 38

Left: *Tate shows his fine bowling action.* Right: *The score of 203 against Northants at Hove in 1921, when Tate and Ted Bowley added 385 for the second wicket, is still the second highest partnership in Sussex's history.*

wickets, a record for a series which endured until it was broken by Alec Bedser in 1953.

He was an excellent hard-hitting batsman as well. Before his bowling transformation he scored 203 against Northamptonshire at Hove in 1921, sharing in a second-wicket partnership of 385 with Ted Bowley, which remains a Sussex record. For the County he passed 1,000 runs in every season between 1919 and 1928 (1,548 in 1927, average 36.00 – his best performance); he took 100 wickets each year between 1922 and 1935, except in 1933 when an injury caused him to end up with only 99; and he did the cricketer's double for Sussex from 1922 to 1928 and, with the help of 100 not out in a Test against South Africa, in 1929 too. His was a quite remarkable record, but he was a fit man who could go on bowling for hours, keeping an immaculate length and seeming to enjoy every moment of the game. In two seasons (1925 and 1934) he bowled more than 1,400 overs for Sussex, in the latter season at the age of thirty-nine. For England he also had an enviable record: 155 wickets in 39 matches (average 26.16) with an economy rate of fractionally over 2 runs per over. Bearing in mind that he was bowling at times against batsmen like Bradman and Ponsford in their pomp, it was a considerable achievement.

Maurice kept playing into the 1937 season when he was by then forty-two years of age. He might, with more foresight, have seen that his powers were beginning to wane, but in any event, he was summoned in August to meet Brigadier D'Arcy Brownlow, chairman of the committee, who told him that his services would no longer be required in 1938 and not even for the remaining matches of 1937. It was clearly the unhappiest day of his life and, as he said later: 'It was not so much what was done, as the way they did it.'

He left Sussex to become a professional for Walsall, served in the army in the Second World War and played again for the County in wartime matches. In 1950 he entered the pub trade, his last pub being at the 'Greyhound' in Wadhurst, where he died in his sixty-first year in 1956.

# N. Ian Thomson
*RHB & RM, 1952-72*

**Born:** Walsall, Staffordshire, 23 January 1929

**County Cap:** 1953

**Batting Record:**

| M | I | NO | Runs | Avge |
|---|---|----|------|------|
| 403 | 558 | 90 | 6,827 | 14.58 |
| *32* | *17* | *5* | *69* | *5.75* |
| **100** | **50** | | **CT/ST** | |
| - | 13 | | 123 | |
| - | - | | *3* | |

**Bowling Record:**

| O | M | Runs | W | Avge |
|---|---|------|---|------|
| 14,027 | 4,246 | 31,186 | 1,527 | 20.42 |
| *298* | *48* | *1,063* | *52* | *20.44* |
| **5wI** | **10wM** | | | |
| 70 | 8 | | | |
| - | - | | | |

**Career Best Performances:**
77 v. Leicestershire, Loughborough, 1959
*16 v. Gloucestershire, Hove, 1971 (GC)*
34.2-19-49-10 v. Warwickshire, Worthing, 1964
*13-5-23-4 v. Warwickshire, Lord's, 1964 (GC final)*
*5-0-23-4 v. Warwickshire, Edgbaston, 1971 (SL)*

The author A.A. Thomson described his namesake, Ian Thomson, at the height of his career for Sussex, thus: 'Sturdy, good-humoured, seemingly tireless, he appears to have been bowling all day; indeed, he appears to have been bowling, if not from the dawn of time, at least from the first day of May, with the intention of going on bowling till the middle of September.' He was, by any standards, a quite remarkable bowler and only Maurice Tate, among Sussex medium-pace bowlers, can perhaps outshine him.

Ian's early days were spent in Essex and at the Forest School he excelled at cricket. After playing for Essex Young Amateurs, he spent two years' National Service in the RAF. His family then moved to Brighton and Ian's allegiance transferred from Essex to Sussex.

He first played as an amateur for Sussex in 1952 and in the early season 'friendly' against Hampshire at Southampton he scored 115 not out at a rapid rate. In his first county match against Northamptonshire, he captured the prized wicket of their prolific Australian, Jock Livingston, and went on to collect another 44 wickets that season. In 1952, he turned professional and captured 101 wickets, receiving his cap from David Sheppard in the September of the following year. From then until 1964, he took 100 wickets in twelve successive seasons and equalled Maurice Tate's record, which was certainly no mean feat.

Ian did not always look like a demon bowler. He had a shuffling and rather unimpressive approach to the wicket, but his right arm came over high and his natural delivery was the in-dipper. On a green top, however, he was able to make the ball leap off the seam almost as if by magic and he had a good leg-cutter in his repertoire. He enjoyed a host of impressive performances: three wickets in four balls against Gloucestershire in 1953 and against Kent in 1957, 8 wickets for 79 against Worcestershire in 1956 and 7 wickets for 12 against Northamptonshire in 1957 (taking 4

*Ian Thomson, despite a rather ungainly approach to the wicket, was a highly effective bowler.*

wickets in 8 balls without conceding a run).

His greatest performances, however, did not come until 1964. In the match against Warwickshire at Worthing in June – a match, incidentally, which the County managed to lose by being dismissed for 23 in their second innings – he captured all 10 of the visitors' wickets in the first innings and he followed this with a further 5 in the second, bowling altogether 59.4 overs with 34 maidens and hauling in 15 for 75. Only Cyril Bland in 1899 had previously taken all ten. Not content with this performance, he waited until the end of the season for another great effort. Sussex had won the first Knock-Out Competition by beating Worcestershire in 1963 and claiming the Gillette Cup, and a year later they were back at Lord's in September, ready to do battle again with Warwickshire, who had so comprehensively demolished them in the Championship match. In the early round matches Ian had bowled well and captured 5 wickets, but nothing compared with what happened at Lord's. Both Ted Dexter and Mike Smith of Warwickshire were generally committed to batting first if they won the toss. Smith won, but it must have been a difficult choice for the morning was hazy and with a start at 10.45 a.m. the ball was bound to wobble about. And it certainly did for Ian! In the first thirty-five minutes he removed his opponents' top three for 21 runs and, although Mike and Alan Smith both reached double figures, the Midlands county were bundled out for 127 and by lunchtime the match was virtually done and dusted. Sussex romped home by 8 wickets. As the *Cricketer* report noted, it was unlikely that the Warwickshire bowlers would have done as well as Ian with his 'accuracy, prodigious movement and cleverly disguised changes of pace' and the award for man of the match was justifiably his.

During Ian's career there were some excellent medium-pace bowlers on the scene – to name but two, Hampshire's Derek Shackleton and Warwickshire's Tom Cartwright – so it was perhaps unsurprising that he did not feature greatly in England's Test plans. He was a member of the MCC 'A' team which toured Pakistan in 1955/56, but he did not play in the representative matches and he had to wait until 1964/65 to make his Test debut in the MCC tour of South Africa. Although he played in all five Tests, there were few wickets that resembled those in England and his 9 wickets cost 63 runs each. Sadly, he did not get another chance, although what he might have achieved under English conditions is another story.

He wanted go out at the top and after the 1965 season he retired. He was pressed back into service for a few matches in 1971 and 1972, but he was by then, at the age of forty-three, well past his best.

# Joseph Vine
*RHB & LB, 1896-1922*

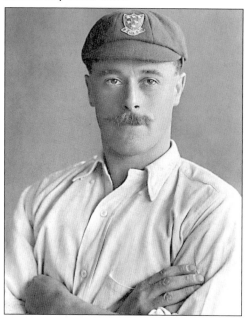

**Born:** Willingdon, 15 May 1875
**Died:** Aldrington, Hove, 25 April 1946

**Batting Record:**

| M | I | NO | Runs | Avge |
|---|---|---|---|---|
| 506 | 858 | 69 | 24,120 | 30.57 |
| **100** | **50** | **CT/ST** | | |
| 33 | 141 | 213 | | |

**Bowling Record:**

| O | M | Runs | W | Avge |
|---|---|---|---|---|
| 6,489 | 1,381 | 17,658 | 621 | 28.43 |
| **5wI** | **10wM** | | | |
| 25 | 3 | | | |

**Career Best Performances:**
202 v. Northamptonshire, Hastings, 1920
25.2-6-68-8 v. Oxford University, Eastbourne, 1906

Joe Vine was the leading professional batsman in Sussex in the first part of the twentieth century, when the County's batting was dominated by brilliant amateurs like Ranji and Charles Fry. Among the professionals, only Ernest Killick and the Relf brothers could hold a candle to him.

Joe was below average height, but well built and extremely agile and, when he first gained his place in the County XI in 1896 at the age of twenty-one, it was, to some extent at least, because of his excellent fielding. His first few seasons with the County saw the batting dominated by Ranji, Fry, Brann, Newham and Murdoch, so his chances were fairly limited, but he scored a maiden century – 115 not out against Hampshire at Hove – in 1899, and his career moved on apace from that point. In 1901, he started to open the batting with Charles Fry and in that season he became the first Sussex player to complete the 'double' when he scored 1,124 runs and took 103 wickets, taking 15 wickets (8 for 76 and 7 for 85) against Nottinghamshire at Trent Bridge. Although he never again took 100 wickets in a season, his leg-breaks remained very much part and parcel of the County attack and he enjoyed some excellent analyses, especially it seems, when bowling against Oxford and Cambridge students.

His batting, however, was a different matter altogether. He passed 1,000 runs in a season on fourteen occasions and his opening partnerships with Charles Fry surely contributed to the County's success in the early part of the twentieth century. Thirty-three times they passed 100 together and on six occasions they went past 200: in 1901 at Hove against Kent they added 216 (Fry 140, Vine 84) and against Cambridge University 203 (Fry 241, Vine 59); in 1902 at Hastings against Surrey 238 (Fry 159, Vine 92), when the County reached what has remained their highest innings total ever of 705 for 8 wickets declared; in 1904 at Hove against Hampshire 287 (Fry 211, Vine 111), against Cambridge University 220 (Fry 150, Vine 82) and against Surrey 202 (Fry 181, Vine 65).

While he was Fry's partner, he acquired the reputation of being something of a slowcoach, and was even compared to a snail in one cartoon, and there is little doubt that he was, to some extent, transformed from a free-hitter into a more defensive player, Fry's advice being that he should not score more than one four per over, but keep one end going and break the bowlers' hearts! Fry may well have been right: a team of such brilliance needed some solidity as well. But it was not only with Charles Fry that he achieved success. He enjoyed 1st-wicket stands

Left: *Joe Vine was also a highly effective leg-spin bowler.* Right: *Joe the Edwardian gentleman on tour with MCC in Australia in 1911/12.*

of 252 and 204 with Robert Relf, a 2nd-wicket stand of 249 with Vallance Jupp, a 3rd-wicket stand also with Robert Relf and a 5th-wicket stand of 207 with Ranji. He also carried his bat through an innings on nine occasions.

After the First World War, Joe returned to Sussex in 1919 and in the next season, at the age of forty-five, he reached his one and only double hundred – 202 against Northamptonshire at Hove, made in just under five hours and, as *Wisden* commented 'playing vigorous cricket all the time'. When Arthur Gilligan, who had just joined Sussex, congratulated him on his knock, he replied quietly: 'I wouldn't have dared do that when C.B. Fry was playing. I once hit three fours in an over and Mr Fry came up to me and told me plainly that it was my job to stay there and leave that sort of cricket to him.'

Joe might have been more prominent in representative cricket but for the role assigned to him by Fry and the fact that, in his time, such talent was on hand that there that was great competition for batting places in England sides, a situation that Ted Bowley found some twenty years later. Only once was Joe selected for the Players versus the Gentlemen and that was not at Lord's, but only at Hastings in 1903, although he did play for teams such as 'Players of the South' against tourists and for 'South' versus 'North'. In 1911/12 a chance came his way when he was a member of the MCC side under Johnny Douglas that toured Australia. He played in two Tests and took part with Frank Woolley, while batting at number eight and scoring 36, in a partnership of 143 for the 7th wicket in the final match. This is still a record 7th-wicket stand for England against Australia.

On retirement in 1922, he coached Ranji's State XI and that of the Maharaja of Cooch Behar in India and then coached at Brighton College, a post he held with distinction for many years.

# Christopher E. Waller

*RHB & SLA, 1974-85*

**Born:** Guildford, Surrey, 3 October 1948

**County Cap:** 1976

**Batting Record:**

| M | I | NO | Runs | Avge |
|---|---|----|------|------|
| 227 | 235 | 98 | 1,308 | 9.54 |
| *143* | *56* | *26* | *221* | *7.37* |
| **100** | **50** | | **CT/ST** | |
| - | 2 | | 120 | |
| *-* | *-* | | *33* | |

**Bowling Record:**

| O | M | Runs | W | Avge |
|---|---|------|---|------|
| 6,293 | 1,824 | 16,117 | 534 | 30.18 |
| *826.4* | *92* | *3,541* | *119* | *29.75* |
| **5wI** | **10wM** | | | |
| 18 | 1 | | | |
| - | - | | | |

**Career Best Performances:**

51* v. Cambridge University, Cambridge, 1981
*18* v. Glamorgan, Hove, 1975 (SL)*
34.3-15-61-7 v. Derbyshire, Derby, 1985
*10-3-25-4 v. Minor Counties (South), Hove, 1975 (B&H)*

Chris Waller, joined the Surrey staff in 1965 at the age of sixteen and, although he performed quite well, especially in 1971, and was capped one year later, too much competition among spinners at the Oval led him to accept Sussex's offer of a contract for 1974. He knew full well that the Hove wicket was not renowned for helping spinners, but he has never been afraid of a challenge.

The hallmark of Chris was that he was a genuine slow spinner. With his classic slow left-armer's action in the authentic, old-fashioned style, he practised deception by guile, was patient, toyed with batsmen until he lured them to destruction and always showed courage when slogged.

His first two years with the County were of steady progress, but in 1976 he started to make great strides, took 71 wickets at less than 26 each and was considered – perhaps only as an outsider as this was the age of Derek Underwood – for the MCC tour of the Indian sub-continent in 1976/77. The following season, he received something of a set-back as he was to some extent supplanted by Giles Cheatle, five years younger than himself and also a slow left-armer who had joined the County at the same time but had shown no form until 1977. Giles then had the more successful season, but in 1978 Chris came back with 40 Championship wickets and headed the County's bowling averages. Despite his success in the longer game, Chris did not get a look-in for limited-overs matches, where Giles performed admirably in the three competitions and was a member of the side that won the Gillette Cup that year. The friendly rivalry continued into 1979, but in 1980, in one of the many ironies that seem to pervade first-class cricket in England, Giles decided to sign for Surrey.

For the next five seasons Chris remained a staple part of the County's spin attack, and in 1982 he bowled out his old county with 7 for 67 at Hove and nearly won the match against Leicestershire with his one and only Championship 50.

Chris has always been a good communicator and has taken a full part in encouraging and coaching younger players. Despite a career best of 7 for 61 against Derbyshire in 1985, he decided to retire at the end of the season and he has remained ever since in various important coaching roles with the County Club, including that of Youth Cricket Director.

# Rupert T. Webb
*RHB & WK, 1948-60*

**Born:** Harrow, Middlesex, 11 July 1922

**County Cap:** 1952

**Batting Record:**

| M | I | NO | Runs | Avge |
|---|---|---|---|---|
| 255 | 331 | 103 | 2,668 | 11.70 |
| **50** | **100** | | **CT/ST** | |
| - | - | | 322/127 | |

**Bowling Record:**

| O | M | Runs | W | Avge |
|---|---|---|---|---|
| 6 | 1 | 43 | 1 | 43.00 |
| **5wI** | **10wM** | | | |
| - | - | | | |

**Career Best Performances:**
49* v. Lancashire, Hove, 1955
4-0-34-1 v. Oxford University, Hove, 1953
Best season 1955: 65 dismissals (ct 41 and st 24)

When Rupert Webb first played for Sussex in 1948 on special registration from Middlesex, he was only the seventh regular County stumper in the ninety-two years from the time when C.H. Ellis started his career in 1856 and passed the gloves onward via Phillips, Butt, Street, Cornford to Billy Griffith. Webb did not immediately succeed Billy, who played on for two more years, but he attracted some favourable comments by *Playfair*, such as 'showing glimpses of real ability', before he began a full career in 1950.

Between 1950 and 1956, he was the County's premier 'keeper, not merely one who did well standing back to the quick bowlers, but an able taker of spinners as well. In 1955, the year when Robin Marlar became captain and took 129 wickets, he stumped 24 batsmen. He was not a top-notch batsman and the 439 runs he scored in 1955 were the most he ever achieved and included his highest score of 49 not out against Lancashire. In 1957, he shared the 'keeping duties with David Mantell and then in 1958 he was injured for part of the season. Jim Parks substituted behind the stumps and did so well that he found his way back to Test cricket in this role. Fortunate as it was for Jim, it heralded the demise of Rupert's career and, after a benefit year in 1960, he retired.

Like Don Smith he had been a soccer referee in the winter and, aged only thirty-eight at the end of the 1960 season, he was an active man needing a job, so he found one in the oil industry and did not retire from this second career until 1980. He was married to actress Barbara Whatley, and when he appeared to be at a loose end in his retirement, she came up with an astonishing suggestion. Why not try to become a male model? A macho sportsman and oil company manager was hardly likely to enthuse immediately at such a proposal, but he engaged an agent and is now forced to admit to success in his third career: 'There are thousands of teenagers in the business competing for work, but only a dozen in my age group with my sort of looks.' It did not stop there either. He went on to play the father of the jilted bride in the film *Four Weddings and a Funeral*: all rather different from taking the bails off!

119

# Alan P. Wells
*RHB & RM, 1981-96*

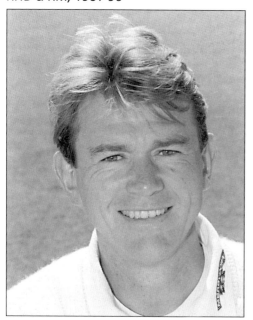

**Born:** Newhaven, 2 October 1961

**County Cap:** 1986
**County Captain:** 1992-1996

**Batting Record:**

| M | I | NO | Runs | Avge |
|---|---|---|---|---|
| 299 | 497 | 70 | 17,135 | 40.12 |
| *302* | *282* | *35* | *7,852* | *31.79* |
| **100** | **50** | | **CT/ST** | |
| 40 | 80 | | 184 | |
| *6* | *52* | | *82* | |

**Bowling Record:**

| O | M | Runs | W | Avge |
|---|---|---|---|---|
| 171 | 25 | 735 | 10 | 73.50 |
| *21.2* | *1* | *142* | *7* | *20.29* |

**Career Best Performances:**
253* v. Yorkshire, Middlesbrough, 1991
*127 v. Hampshire, Portsmouth, 1993 (SL)*
13-0-67-3 v. Worcestershire, Worcester, 1987
*0.1-0-0-1 v. Glamorgan, Cardiff, 1987 (SL)*

There were few better batsmen in England than Alan Wells in the seven seasons from 1989 to 1995. In that period, he made 10,157 runs (average 48.60) for Sussex and scored 30 hundreds. His only international recognition during that period consisted of two England 'A' tours (where he was successively vice-captain and captain), one limited-overs international and one solitary Test cap. This was at a time when players like Matthew Maynard and Mark Lathwell were winning Test places and scarcely scoring a run between them. That Alan was not invited to tour South Africa in the winter of 1995/96 after his one Test match against the West Indies in 1995 almost beggars belief.

Alan, eighteen months younger than his brother Colin, came to Sussex in 1982 at the age of twenty and made 63 against Cambridge University in his initial first-class innings. After a period of acclimatisation he scored his first hundred in 1984 – 105 not out against Leicestershire – and reached 1,000 runs for the County. Two seasons later he scored a sparkling 150 not out against Nottinghamshire, adding 149 with Tony Pigott and saving the match for the County, while in 1987, in the County's match with Kent, he joined his brother in an unbeaten partnership of 303 in which he made 161 not out with 3 sixes and 19 fours and Colin

reached 140 not out. This stand beat the fifty-year-old record of partnerships between Sussex brothers which Jim and Harry Parks had achieved against Hampshire in 1937.

He led the Sussex batting averages in 1989 and was ninth in the national averages and his 'purple patch' had begun. The 1991 season saw him record 1,784 runs at an average of over 60, which included an innings of 253 not out in 406 minutes with 3 sixes and 27 fours in the County's defeat of Yorkshire by an innings, and the recording by Alan of the highest score by a Sussex batsman against the Tykes, beating Charles Fry's 234 which had been made at Bradford as long ago as 1903. In 1993, when the Australians were touring, he made 93 against them at Hove, but some lesser mortals seemed to find their way into the England team. In early 1990, he unwisely joined Mike Gatting's 'rebel' English XI in South Africa, but happily escaped any ban and in 1993/94 he was made vice-captain of England 'A' in South Africa and captain of the team in the following winter when they were in India.

In 1992, arguably leap-frogging over his brother, he was appointed Sussex captain and

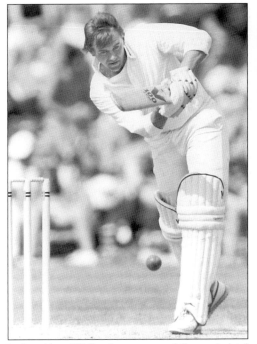

Left: *Alan Wells drives powerfully and* (right) *shows his square cut.* (George Herringshaw *www.sporting-heroes.net*)

his run of excellent form continued, while in the first three years of his captaincy the County reached the acceptable, if not outstanding, positions of 7th, 10th and 8th in the Championship. At the same time the County reached the final of the NatWest Trophy in 1993. This season might well be seen as the high point of Alan's career. In the semi-final match, against Glamorgan at Hove, Sussex, facing their opponents' total of 220 in 60 overs, were themselves 110 for 6 wickets in the 45th over, but Alan, joined by Neil Lenham, scored 106 and saw them home with 4 balls to spare with what *Wisden* described as 'a brilliant one-day innings in which he manipulated the bowling masterfully.' On one occasion, as the Glamorgan spinner Robert Croft saw him backing away towards square leg, the bowler fired the ball further down the leg side, only to see Alan move back to the off and a wide be called.

The 1993 NatWest final was certainly a classic. Sussex recorded an excellent 321 for 6 wickets in their 60 overs only to see Warwickshire edge past them on the very last ball to reach the highest team total achieved in

a limited-overs final. But, sadly, there were rumblings about the captaincy. Some said that the Warwickshire players were amazed at Sussex's field-placings and the discontent, although muted for some two further seasons, continued into the 1995 and 1996 seasons when the County finished 15th and 12th in the Championship. Matters were not improved by Alan's book, *The Captain's Year*, in which he appeared to criticise two of his team, Martin Speight and Ian Salisbury, while others suggested that the captain was short on inspiration and the dressing-room atmosphere was unhappy. When Alan returned from a Barbados benefit tour in early 1997, he found that the committee had sacked him. It might have been the right decision, but the way in which it was handled was in the sad Sussex tradition – inept and unfeeling. Not wanting to serve under another captain, Alan was released from his contract and joined Kent on a five-year deal. Sadly, he never reproduced his real form for his adopted county and towards the end of his contract found himself more often out than in the Kent Championship team.

# Colin M. Wells

*RHB & RM, 1979-93*

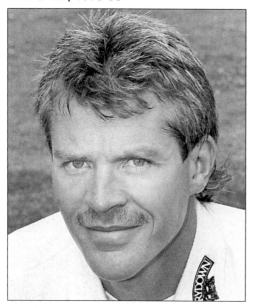

**Born:** Newhaven, 3 March 1960

**County Cap:** 1982

**Batting Record:**

| M | I | NO | Runs | Avge |
|---|---|----|------|------|
| 272 | 430 | 69 | 12,310 | 34.09 |
| *264* | *239* | *33* | *5,401* | *26.22* |
| **100** | **50** | | **CT/ST** | |
| 21 | 58 | | 84 | |
| *4* | *23* | | *59* | |

**Bowling Record:**

| O | M | Runs | W | Avge |
|---|---|------|---|------|
| 4,690 | 1,098 | 13,241 | 392 | 33.77 |
| *1576.5* | *146* | *5,777* | *178* | *32.46* |
| **5wI** | **10wM** | | | |
| 7 | - | | | |
| *4* | *-* | | | |

**Career Best Performances:**
203 v. Hampshire, Hove, 1984
*117 v. Glamorgan, Swansea, 1989 (B&H)*
20.4-8-42-7 v. Derbyshire, 1991
*4-0-15-4 v. Worcestershire, Worcester, 1983 (SL)*

Joining Sussex, aged nineteen, in 1979, Colin Wells took little time to get into his stride and in 1980 soon attracted the nickname 'Bomber' owing to his early explosive appearances. *Wisden* of 1981 commented: 'Wells' team-mates did not nickname him "Bomber" for nothing. He gave the ball a terrific whack, hitting numerous 6s over mid-wicket and passing 1,000 runs in his first full season. Long before the end of the summer critics were rating him as a youngster with Test potential.'

It is well known that, even after early batting promise, the wily old pros on the county circuit soon start to find a player out. This was perhaps true of Colin. 1981 proved to be a far less productive season for him, although he was back in the groove with 1,248 runs and three hundreds in the next season. 1983 saw a significant development of his medium-pace bowling with his easy, rhythmic run-up, and from then until 1990 he was effectively the County's leading all-rounder, scoring 1,000 runs in another four seasons and getting close in most others, while taking 40 or 50 wickets at the same time. In 1984, he reached 203 against Hampshire and scored four other centuries and, three seasons later, he made 1,456 runs (average 45.50) and another five hundreds. On the bowling front he took seven wickets in an innings three times: 7 for 42 against Derbyshire

in 1991 and 7 for 65 against Kent and 7 for 82 against Surrey in 1989. One of his most pleasurable achievements was in 1987 when the Wells brothers broke the fifty-year old partnership for Sussex brothers made by Jim and Harry Parks in 1937 by putting on an unbroken 303 against Kent, Colin's own share being 140 with two 6s and seventeen 4s.

The Test call-up, sadly, never materialised. His form in limited-overs cricket had always been outstanding and in 1985, when Colin was chosen for the England one-day squad to play in Sharjah, one newspaper thought he was about to claim Botham's England spot. No such luck! He played in two limited-overs matches, scoring 17 and 5 and not bowling.

In 1992 his form tailed off. He had been county vice-captain from 1988 to 1990 and, when his younger brother Alan inherited the captaincy in 1992, he sought fresh pastures and moved to Derbyshire for three years before going to Somerset CCC as coach. He has now returned to Derbyshire as Second XI coach.

# Albert F. (Bert) Wensley
*RHB & RMF, 1922-36*

**Born:** Brighton, 24 May 1898
**Died:** Ware, Hertfordshire, 17 June 1970

**Batting Record:**

| M | I | NO | Runs | Avge |
|---|---|----|------|------|
| 373 | 552 | 61 | 9,807 | 19.97 |

| 100 | 50 | | CT/ST | |
|-----|----|--|-------|--|
| 8 | 39 | | 249/1 | |

**Bowling Record:**

| O | M | Runs | W | Avge |
|---|---|------|---|------|
| 11,537 | 2,874 | 28,187 | 1,067 | 26.41 |

| 5wI | 10wM | | | |
|-----|------|--|--|--|
| 53 | 9 | | | |

**Career Best Performances:**
140 v. Glamorgan, Swansea, 1928
23-9-41-8 v. Leicestershire, Eastbourne, 1933

Playing in the shadow of the Maurice Tate and being much the same sort of cricketer did not stop Bert Wensley from becoming a wholly effective medium-fast bowler and an aggressive batsman. He left school at fifteen to serve an apprenticeship in a Glasgow shipyard before first playing for Sussex in 1922; by then he was twenty-four and Maurice was well established in the Sussex team. It was not until three years later, however, that he started to make his mark with nearly 900 runs and 109 wickets, which included an unusual happening when he and Maurice bowled unchanged throughout both Glamorgan innings. Although Maurice's 14 wickets were by far the lion's share, Bert's performance of 4 for 52 off 35 overs was by no means negligible. The following season was an anti-climax as he made over 100 runs fewer and took only 37 wickets and 'for a man who had given promise of being considered for high honours' according to *Wisden* 'this failure was indeed surprising.'

This was nothing more than a blip and 1927 saw him score his maiden hundred, reach 1,000 runs for the first time and take 79 wickets. The following season was even better, when he reached 1,581 runs and, batting at number three, made 140 against Glamorgan and two further centuries besides. In 1929, he completed the only double of his career with 1,057 runs and 113 wickets, including 14 in the match against Northamptonshire and, a year later, when poor form had caused his demotion to number ten in the batting order, he responded with a remarkable display of powerful hitting and in 110 minutes scored 120 out of 178 for the 9th wicket against Derbyshire. Bert produced many other singular performances: 8 wickets in an innings on five occasions, a hat-trick against Middlesex in 1935, 80 in 40 minutes against Kent at Hastings in 1931, 5 catches in an innings on two occasions, but what perhaps stands more than all this is the work-load he happily carried – in seven of his eleven important seasons for Sussex he bowled well over 1,000 overs in each – a real glutton for work!

Like many professionals, he spent some of his winters abroad – in Madras and also in New Zealand, where he succeeded Ted Bowley at Auckland, for whom in 1929/30 he took 9 for 36 against Otago. After he retired in 1936, he became involved in coaching, most notably at Haileybury College between 1950 and 1963.

# Kepler C. Wessels
*LHB & OB, 1976-80*

**Born:** Bloemfontein, South Africa, 14 September 1957

**County Cap:** 1977

**Batting Record:**

| M | I | NO | Runs | Avge |
|---|---|----|------|------|
| 53 | 94 | 11 | 4,329 | 52.16 |
| *40* | *40* | *1* | *1,411* | *36.18* |
| **100** | **50** | | **CT/ST** | |
| 10 | 28 | | 42 | |
| *2* | *10* | | *16* | |

**Bowling Record:**

| O | M | Runs | W | Avge |
|---|---|------|---|------|
| 4 | 0 | 11 | 0 | -- |

**Career Best Performances:**
254 v. Middlesex, Hove, 1980
*106 v. Nottinghamshire, Hove, 1977 (B&H)*

Sussex people will always regret that Kepler Wessels was able to play a meagre five seasons for the County and take a full part in only two. Of those batsmen who played solely after the Second World War, he must rank among the County's very best. While still at Grey College in South Africa he made his debut, aged sixteen, for Orange Free State and, although felled by the second delivery he received, he nevertheless went on to reach a determined 32. He came to Sussex in 1976, playing in only two matches, and anyone who was fortunate enough to see him at the age of nineteen play the ferocious Wayne Daniel in the West Indies fixture at Hove and go on to 55 not out would have recognised that a future star was on the horizon.

In 1977, he played in nine games and in his 500 runs in that season was a fine first hundred – 138 not out against Kent. National Service in South Africa and a knee injury restricted his progress in 1978, but in the next two seasons he displayed his full ability and led the Sussex Championship averages in both seasons. In 1979, he made 1,800 runs in all

County matches and, with an average of nearly 53, he was in sixth place in the national averages and the scorer of six hundreds. In the following season he was even more successful, ranking in third place in the national averages at 65 runs per innings. In the course of the season he produced two massive innings, 197 not out against Nottinghamshire and 254 against Middlesex. In the latter match, Sussex had been dismissed for 172 in their first innings and had been forced to follow on, but Kepler defied the visitors' strong attack for six hours, hitting 29 fours and 3 sixes and thereby saving the game.

Sussex at this time had something of an embarrassment of riches, with Imran Khan, Garth le Roux and Kepler all registered and only two able to play in Championship matches. Wessels had been involved in World Series Cricket in 1978/79 and had played for Queensland, so it was perhaps no surprise when he emigrated to Australia, married an Australian and in 1982 started playing Test cricket for his adopted country. A somewhat controversial career finally led him back to South Africa, where he became the first Test captain of his country after their re-admission to world cricket.

# Herbert L. Wilson
*RHB & OB, 1913-24*

**Born:** Cottesbrooke, Northamptonshire, 27 June 1881
**Died:** Halland, Uckfield, 15 March 1937

**County Captain:** 1919-1921

**Batting Record:**

| M | I | NO | Runs | Avge |
|---|---|---|---|---|
| 140 | 256 | 12 | 6,138 | 25.15 |
| **100** | **50** | | **CT/ST** | |
| 6 | 18 | | 56 | |

**Bowling Record:**

| O | M | Runs | W | Avge |
|---|---|---|---|---|
| 257 | 18 | 1,229 | 26 | 47.26 |
| **5wI** | **10wM** | | | |
| - | - | | | |

**Career Best Performances:**
187 v. Warwickshire, Hove, 1920
6.5-0-19-4 v. Nottinghamshire, Eastbourne, 1920

Born in the Midlands, but educated at Framlingham College in Suffolk, Herbert Wilson played for the Minor County for eight seasons before coming to Sussex in 1913. The fine form he had already shown was translated into immediate success as an opening batsman in Sussex. He did not score his maiden century until the end of the season, in the remarkable match with Gloucestershire which the County won easily. In the first innings Herbert (109) and Robert Relf (113) and in the second Joe Vine (101) and Albert Relf (117) so dominated the scoring that no other player exceeded 30 apart from C.O.H. Sewell's 63 in the visitors' second knock. At the end of the season, Herbert had amassed 1,352 runs and, at the age of thirty-two, was almost certainly the oldest man to score 1,000 runs in his debut season.

He batted well in 1914 and, when cricket resumed after the First World War, he was invited to captain the County. His own batting, with runs scored primarily in front of the wicket – with, according to *Wisden*, 'plenty of power and a fine style' – continued to prosper, although number four rather than the opener's slot was now his regular position. In the following season he made his highest score for Sussex – 187

against Warwickshire, in which he hit 23 fours. Although he remained captain in 1921, he found it increasingly hard to get away from his business and his batting suffered, although he remained a popular captain. He was only an occasional bowler, but every dog is said to have his day, and Herbert's occurred in the match with Nottinghamshire at Eastbourne in 1920. Sussex had batted poorly in both innings and the Midlands side only needed 29 to win. Opening the bowling with Ted Bowley, he disposed of the first four batsmen in no time at all and the visitors, having changed their batting order and allowed most of the team to leave the ground, were in a highly embarrassing situation with opener Lee (in a loud pink shirt) and number eleven Richmond guiding them home as the Nottinghamshire skipper, Arthur Carr, dressed in a lounge suit, looked on apprehensively.

Herbert Wilson's other important contribution to Sussex cricket was his insistence as a captain on a high standard of fielding, a tradition which his successor as skipper, Arthur Gilligan, took over and improved. Herbert relinquished the captaincy after 1921, but played for the County occasionally until the end of 1924.

# John Wisden
*RHB & RF/RM, 1845-63*

**Born:** Brighton, 5 September 1826
**Died:** Westminster, London, 5 April 1884

**Batting Record:**

| M | I | NO | Runs | Avge |
|---|---|----|------|------|
| 82 | 148 | 17 | 2,234 | 17.05 |
| 100 | CT/ST | | | |
| 2 | 83 | | | |

**Bowling Record:**

| Runs | W | Avge | Other wickets |
|------|---|------|---------------|
| 3,647 | 350 | 10.42 | 230 |
| 5wI | 10wM (including 'other wickets') | | |
| 61 | 21 | | |

**Career Best Performances:**
148 v. Yorkshire, Bramall Lane, Sheffield, 1855
8-24 v. MCC, Lord's 1859

John Wisden was described in his obituary in the 1885 edition of his almanack as 'a splendid all-round cricketer in his day: a good bat, a fine field, and as a bowler unsurpassed. A quiet, unassuming, and thoroughly upright man. A fast friend and a generous employer.'

His father, Thomas, was a builder in Brighton. After his father's death he went to work for Tom Box, the Sussex wicketkeeper, who was the proprietor of the Egremont Hotel. It was through this connection that he was introduced to cricket and he played the game whenever he could. Even at this early age, he had an eye for business and he was prepared to bowl or field for his seniors whenever they needed assistance.

There have been a number of unflattering descriptions of John's size – 'a little gnome of a man' was one – and he was certainly diminutive, probably little more than 5ft 4in tall and never weighing much more than seven stone in his youth. But whatever his apparent physical disadvantages, he became one of the great fast bowlers of his time, delivering his round arm at a brisk pace, with its 'very fast and ripping deliveries'. He first played for Sussex in 1845, taking 6 wickets for 46 in the first Kent innings and 3 for 59 in the second. Records at that time were not kept accurately, but it would seem that in all matches between 1848 and 1859 he averaged 225 wickets per season, therefore totalling some 2,700. In 1850, playing for the North against the South, he took all ten wickets clean bowled, a feat that remains unparalleled. He was also a sound and correct batsman, who favoured the 'draw' shot, and his 148 against Yorkshire in 1855 was the only first-class century of the season.

He also played for William Clarke's All England side and, when he fell out with Clarke, for his own United England XI. In 1859, he toured North America with George Parr and is credited with taking 6 wickets in six deliveries against XXII of Canada and the USA.

In 1855, together with Frederick Lillywhite, he set up a cricketing and cigar business in New Coventry Street, London and, after he ended his career with Sussex in 1863, he was involved in launching the *Cricketer's Almanack*, which bore his name. He later owned a cigar shop in Cranbourn Street, off Leicester Square, where he lived until 1884 when he died of cancer. He was well named 'The Little Wonder.'

# D. James (Jim) Wood
*RHB & LFM, 1936-55*

**Born:** Horsted Keynes, 19 May 1914
**Died:** Horsted Keynes, 12 March 1989

**County Cap:** 1938

**Batting Record:**

| M | I | NO | Runs | Avge |
|---|---|----|------|------|
| 213 | 250 | 72 | 1,304 | 7.32 |
| 50 | 100 | | CT/ST | |
| - | - | | 89 | |

**Bowling Record:**

| O | M | Runs | W | Avge |
|---|---|------|---|------|
| 6,367 | 1,405 | 18,084 | 585 | 30.91 |
| 5wI | 10wM | | | |
| 21 | 1 | | | |

**Career Best Performances:**
42 v. Nottinghamshire, Trent Bridge, 1951
15.2-6-24-7 v. Middlesex, Hove, 1949

Jim Wood was a real Sussex man and when he died in 1989 he had been living in the same house in the village of Horsted Keynes for forty-two years. Apart from service in the Royal Navy in the Second World War and, of course, playing cricket for Sussex, he rarely ventured from the village where, as a youngster, he had grown up and learned to play all his cricket and football.

He joined Sussex in 1936 at the age of twenty-one and, two years later, he took 52 wickets, including 7 for 52 against Hampshire at Horsham, which he regarded as his favourite ground. 'A pitch I would have liked to carry around with me,' he is once reported as saying. Towards the end of the season he also bagged 7 wickets in the match against the Australians. When he returned from the war the Sussex coaches thought that he might be a replacement for James Langridge who was thought – wrongly as it happened – to be ending his career. Slow left-arm bowling did not prove a success and the first two seasons of the post-war period brought him few wickets, but in 1948 Billy Griffith and Hugh Bartlett encouraged him to return to what he did best and, bowling fast medium round the wicket with a quick nip of the pitch, he gave his career a new lease of life.

In 1949, he bowled nearly 1,000 overs in all matches, took 84 wickets, and in the Bank Holiday match at Hove, with 7 wickets for 24 runs, completely destroyed Middlesex, who lost their first match of the season and limped back to Lord's beaten by 6 wickets. Although he faltered slightly in 1950, he came back strongly in the early 1950s, collared 103 wickets in 1952 – the first Sussex bowler to reach that total since 1939 – and, repeating his dominance over Middlesex three years earlier, he again dismissed seven batsmen, this time for 31 runs. In 1953, when the County gained second place in the Championship under David Sheppard's inspired leadership, Jim was again in the forefront of the attack and took 79 wickets.

At the end of the 1955 season, having enjoyed a well-earned benefit in the Kent match at Hastings, he retired from first-class cricket. He joined a Crawley club as groundsman and player-coach and then served for seven years on the first-class umpires' list before going as head groundsman and cricket coach at Ardingly College.

# Richard A. (Dick) Young
*RHB & WK, 1905-25*

**Born:** Dharwar, India, 16 September 1885
**Died:** Hastings, 1 July 1968

**Batting Record:**

| M | I | NO | Runs | Avge |
|---|---|----|------|------|
| 86 | 148 | 9 | 3,982 | 28.64 |
| **100** | **50** | | **CT/ST** | |
| 6 | 23 | | 72/17 | |

**Bowling Record:**

| O | M | Runs | W | Avge |
|---|---|------|---|------|
| 16 | 2 | 61 | 2 | 31.00 |

**Career Best Performances:**
220 v. Essex, Leyton, 1905
9-1-32-2 v. Surrey, Hastings, 1923

Richard Young, Dick to his friends, was one of the few bespectacled players to represent England at both cricket and amateur Association football. As a schoolboy he gained a high reputation as a batsman/wicketkeeper at Repton School and he then won a blue in 1905 as a freshman at Cambridge University. He played against Oxford in all his four summers, scoring 150 out of 360 in 1906 and captaining the side in 1908. He started playing for Sussex in his first year at Cambridge and his maiden hundred for the County was also his highest, 220 against Essex at Leyton, which was made in four and a half hours. *Wisden* in its report on Sussex's season commented that he had 'such a straight bat and so many ways of scoring that his future ought to be very bright'. In fact, the constraints of his career as a mathematics and cricket master at Eton College for thirty years meant that his appearances for the County were rather sporadic.

In 1907, he played for the Gentlemen against the Players and in the following winter he was a member of the MCC team that toured Australia, playing in two Tests as a wicketkeeper/batsman, although with no great success. He played for the County occasionally between 1908 and 1911 and then became a schoolmaster; he did not appear again in first-class cricket until after the First World War. He headed the County's Championship averages in 1920, and in 1921 he took 124 off the powerful and well-nigh all-conquering Australian touring team in a four-hour innings with 15 fours, scored mainly in front of the wicket. *Wisden* noted that 'he faced Gregory and McDonald with the utmost confidence', which was quite an achievement, given that they took 120 and 150 wickets respectively during the summer! From then until his retirement he played only in the school holidays, although there were times when he displaced the regular professional 'keeper behind the stumps. Despite his inability to play as frequently as he might have wished, he remained a fanatical theorist about the game and wrote a pamphlet, *Time for Experiment*, in which he suggested that captains should have the right to pour 100 gallons of water on any part of the pitch!

Richard was also an adept footballer. A speedy outside-right, he played for both Cambridge University and the Corinthians. He won an amateur international cap against Hungary and also played for the Amateur FA XI against France.